D1072239

No Neutral Ground

DISCARDED

No Neutral Ground

Standing By the Values We Prize in Higher Education

Robert B. Young

Jossey-Bass Publishers • San Francisco

BOWLING GREEN STATE
UNIVERSITY LIBRARIES

Copyright © 1997 by Jossey-Bass Inc., Publishers, 350 Sansome Street, San Francisco, California 94104.

All rights reserved. No part of this publication may be reproduced, stored in a retrieval system, or transmitted, in any form or by any means, electronic, mechanical, photocopying, recording, or otherwise, without the prior written permission of the publisher.

Substantial discounts on bulk quantities of Jossey-Bass books are available to corporations, professional associations, and other organizations. For details and discount information, contact the special sales department at Jossey-Bass Inc., Publishers (415) 433–1740; Fax (800) 605–2665.

For sales outside the United States, please contact your local Simon & Schuster International office.
Jossey-Bass Web address: http://www.josseybass.com

 Manufactured in the United States of America on Lyons Falls Turin Book. This paper is acid-free and 100 percent totally chlorine-free.

Library of Congress Cataloging-in-Publication Data

Young, Robert B., date.
    No neutral ground : standing by the values we prize in higher education / Robert B. Young. — 1st ed.
    p. cm. — (The Jossey-Bass higher and adult education series)
    Includes bibliographical references and index.
    ISBN 0–7879–0800–2 (cloth : acid-free paper)
    1. Education, Higher—Aims and objectives—United States.
    2. Values—Study and teaching (Higher)—United States.
    I. Title. II. Series.
LA227.4.Y68 1997
    378.73—dc20
                                         96–35693

FIRST EDITION
HB Printing   10 9 8 7 6 5 4 3 2 1

The Jossey-Bass
Higher and Adult Education Series

Contents

*This book is dedicated to everyone who has helped me
through a recent major illness: to my family, especially my
wife, Vicky; my son, Peter; and my mother, Alice; to my
friends, students, and colleagues—I shall never find words
deep enough to express my gratitude for their love and
concern; and to my physician, Dr. Janet Bay, whose head,
hands, and heart have enabled me to return to health.*

Preface

> *The things in civilization we most prize are not of*
> *ourselves. They exist by grace of the doings and sufferings*
> *of the continuous human community in which we are a*
> *link. Ours is the responsibility of conserving, transmitting,*
> *rectifying, and expanding the heritage of values we have*
> *received that those that come after us may receive it more*
> *solid and secure, more widely accessible and more*
> *generously shared than we have received it.*
> JOHN DEWEY, 1934, P. 87.

These words appear on the gravestone of John Dewey, who lies beside the chapel at the University of Vermont. Some visitors to the gravesite might walk away uninspired, deaf to the clarion words. Other visitors might simply shake their heads. Yes, they have received many values, but which ones need to be conserved, transmitted, and rectified? What do we *most* prize?

It is difficult to say. The values of higher education are clouded by its functions. The academy is a repository, a generator, and a transmitter of knowledge, as all familiar with it know. It is also a way station for the upwardly mobile, a museum, a library, a public servant (or a public bane during some election years), a bestower of honoraries, a haven for misanthropes, a place to meet life partners, a way to keep people off unemployment lines, an agency for socialization, a social critic, and an instrument of social reform. Each of these functions contains values that are transmitted directly and indirectly by the institution.

Any institution transmits values every day. The academy is no exception. However, the academy is not just any institution; it helps determine the beliefs and behaviors of American society, so it is especially important that higher education be clear and consistent about its values. Trustees must understand the genealogy of values in the academy and, thus, why some policies are easier to enact than others. Administrators must remember their calling—to maintain the meaning of their institutions. And, perhaps to the consternation of these two groups, faculty must rekindle their orneriness, in order to be true to the values of their secular church.

Trustees should be able to develop wiser policy if they understand the values of higher education and how the ideas of the academy can differ from the necessities of the institutions they oversee. For example, trustees must explore the relationships between service, truth, and academic freedom in order to understand why a certain amount of discord is necessary to keep the institution humming. And because so many trustees are good capitalists, they must know how the values of their own enterprise differ from—or mesh with—those of students, administrators, and faculty.

Administrators can be comforted by the clarity that values offer in complex situations. Values underlie every memo or mission statement that administrators produce. Understanding values explains conflicts; aligning values moves institutions forward. And moving institutions forward is, in the end, a solitary endeavor—one that can be performed only when an administrator knows what values are in conflict and why he or she must act to fulfill the values we prize.

Values also differentiate administrators' responsibilities from those of faculty, so perhaps both groups might understand their central meaning by exploring their values. For example, instead of arguing about the facts of their functions—teaching, research, and service—faculty might explore the value concepts within those functions. Great teachers and great researchers might prize truth with equal fervor, but they might have very different opinions about the other values that they, and their institutions, prize.

My central purpose in writing this book was to describe seven essential values and to discuss the ways in which these values can be transmitted with integrity by colleges and universities. That purpose has been shared by other authors. Some have written about academic values such as objectivity and tolerance (for example, Morrill, 1981), and others have brought attention to democratic values such as diversity and justice (for example, Amundson, 1991). One author notes the importance of transcendent values such as fidelity and forgiveness (Rogers, 1989), but another cautions that such transcendent values are too presumptuous; the academy should stick with middle-sized moral values such as sensitivity and sportsmanship (Smith, 1970).

In this book, I describe the following values: service, truth, freedom, individuation, equality, justice, and community—values that have been tested in several different studies. Surveys of private higher education, cabinet administrators, department chairs, student affairs leaders, and nursing educators have supported the notion that all seven values are essential in the academy (American Association of Colleges of Nursing, 1986; Young and Elfrink, 1990; Withers, 1993; Morris, 1994).

Overview of the Contents

This book is divided into three parts. The first part concerns the essential values of the academy and their relationships to the concerns of scholarship and democracy. The second part presents values that challenge those that we prize, and the third part shows ways in which higher education can implement its essential values with integrity.

Part One, "Values We Prize," begins with a chapter about the centrality of values. Values form the basic identity of any college or university; they embody what the institution represents to the public—a public that questions increasingly what the academy is and does. Unfortunately, the academy has not responded adequately to questions about its identity and to accusations that it does not serve society. It needs to shed its stance as a "values neutral" agency, determine its values, present them to the public, and manifest them more effectively.

In the second chapter, I describe the value of service, which can also be called altruism—service that is primarily selfless. However, there is little purism in this definition. The notion of selflessness is qualified by the adjective "primarily." Academicians have to eat, but their work must be more than a means to fill their stomachs. It must be *primarily* altruistic.

I write in the third chapter about the value of truth, which many define as "faithfulness to fact." Truth has been viewed both as an end of the academy and as a means of serving society. Our conceptions of truth have evolved from a focus on the powers of the mind, to the study of observable data, to the usefulness of truth. Each of these focuses has affected the conception and delivery of this value in higher education, for example, from teaching truth to creating it.

The fourth chapter examines the value of freedom, the capacity to exercise choice. Academic freedom has been split into separate rights for professors and students, but professorial freedoms have been emphasized in the American concept of academic freedom. The chapter relates the value of freedom to faculty functions, administrative duties, institutional autonomy, and student rights. Notions of political correctness are related to free speech and to political activities within the academy.

Equality is the subject of the next chapter of the book. Science holds that everything must be treated as equal until proven unequal, creating a tentativeness and fairness inherent in the treatment of the "other" before judgment. Different opinions about equal opportunities and outcomes are examined, as are the notions of equality, meritocracy, and elitism.

Individuation is the subject of the sixth chapter. Individuation means human dignity growing. The primary educational goal of the academy is to differentiate a whole, responsible person from the mass and, thus, to enable that person to create more meaningful bonds with others.

Justice—the subject of Chapter Seven—is essential fairness. It has legal and moral dimensions. Justice balances our social obligations with our individual rights. I examine the obligations of the academy to provide due process, fairer opportunities, and substantial changes to increase the fairness of American social justice.

The value of community is the subject of the eighth chapter. The term *community* can be applied to a physical place, political unit, or spirit of connection among people. That spirit of connection is most important to higher education. It contains two major elements—a sense of mutuality among the residents of the community and a sense of empowerment from residing in the community. Therefore, community is defined here as mutual empowerment.

In the ninth chapter, I consider the relationships among these essential values of the academy. Two clusters of values are described, values that relate to scholarship and to democracy. Values priorities are considered.

Part Two, "Challenges to Our Values," begins with a chapter about capitalism, one of three value systems that challenge the academy. Many students are unabashedly capitalistic. They want the material and personal rewards that study offers them in our society. The excesses of capitalist values are contrasted with the bourgeois virtues that a democracy can generate, such as altruistic egoism, individual enterprise, and bourgeois community.

The eleventh and twelfth chapters describe the challenger values of spirituality and aesthetics. The academy has focused on the generation and sharing of rational truths, one of the major concerns of philosophy, but the other fundamental concerns of philosophy are metaphysics and aesthetics, the ultimate values of good and beauty. Both apprehend that truth contains more than thought can imagine.

The thirteenth chapter concludes my discussion of the challenger values. It examines the push and draw among these and the academic values, and it describes the ebb and flow of values priorities in society. At times, different values will come to the fore, only to retreat later.

Part Three, "Advancing the Values We Prize," includes chapters on identity and the development of integrity. The chapter on identity contains suggestions for manifesting each value. Integrity is more than simply declaring one's loyalty to any values. It is a deliberate attempt to act on those values within a specific context.

Acknowledgments

I would like to thank the following people for their contributions to the development and completion of this book: LuAnn Linson Coldwell, of the Northeastern Ohio Universities College of Medicine; Michael Schwartz, former president of Kent State University; Shirley Smith, also of Kent State University; Bill Crowley and Andrea Ward of Ohio University; Fr. Ian Pac-Urar, Presentation of Our Lord Church; Dennis Golden, president of Fontbonne College; and Gale Erlandson and Rachel Livsey of Jossey-Bass.

The Author

Robert B. Young is professor of education and coordinator of educational leadership at Ohio University. He earned his A.B. degree in history (1965) at the University of Rochester, his M.S. degree in counseling at California State University at Los Angeles (1967), and his Ph.D. degree in higher education (1975) at the University of Illinois, Champaign-Urbana. He has been employed as an administrator in several community colleges, as a research associate at Cornell University, and as a professor at the University of Connecticut, the University of Vermont, Kent State University, and Ohio University.

Young's major research activities have focused on issues of values, administration, student affairs administration, and community colleges. He has written many articles and edited several books on these topics including *Identifying and Implementing the Essential Values of the Profession* (New Directions for Student Services, no. 61, 1993). A frequent keynoter at national and regional conferences, he has served as well on the executive boards of the American College Personnel Association and the National Association of Student Personnel Administrators.

No Neutral Ground

Chapter One

Who Are We?:
Finding Our Identity in Values

Who are you? The question looks simple until we have to answer it. Who am I? An adult would pause before answering, but a child would not hesitate at all. At age eight, I would have said, "Who am I? I'm Bobby Young, and I'm in fourth grade, and I live at 2937 Macklem Avenue." Name, rank, and serial number—that would have been my answer. Today, the question gets more deliberation. The question probes *what* I am and *what* I do, but even more, *who* I am. The answer explains my core, my reasons for being; it dredges my values. But before I answer, I want to know, Who is asking? The answer to that question dictates the detail, breadth, and implications of my self-disclosure.

Far more people are concerned about the identity of higher education today than about the identity of most authors, whatever their age. Who is asking? Everybody is asking, from a spate of politicians and taxpayers to educators themselves. The politicians and the people want facts, not philosophy. They care more about the cost and privilege of higher education than its mission, and many of them do not feel friendly toward the enterprise:

"Did you hear about the professor who was mowing his lawn at 2 P.M.? He's teaching one class a semester; what is he getting paid for?"

"My kids are grown. Why should I pay more taxes for higher education?"

"Why should I hire a person with a liberal arts degree to work on an assembly line?"

Public higher education competes with prisons and welfare and Medicaid for state dollars, and the academy appears elitist just standing on the same stage with these everyday interests. Some states have cut their budgets for higher education so much that public institutions that were once proud to be state *supported* complain that they are now only state *assisted* or perhaps even just state *located*.

Who are you?, the public asks the academy, but an acceptable answer does not fly from her lips as easily as in the past. Since the academy cannot give a quick and satisfactory response, higher education becomes anything that its opponents want to make it—and that seems to be, essentially, more efficient. It can downsize. It can do more with less and let business folk run the enterprise. And although this call for efficiency should prompt a full-fledged discussion of what higher education is as well as what it does, most of the critics do not care that much. They say, "Do whatever you do, so long as you cut your budgets."

The question Who are you? has implications beyond the individual, whether asked of a child or an institution. When the Caterpillar in Wonderland asked Alice Lidell, "Who Are You?" Alice could not come up with an answer, even though she was the only person with common sense in all of Lewis Carroll's book. If Alice could not understand herself, then she could not help her nation understand itself, which was the role that Carroll intended for her to have (Auden, 1962).

In the same way, higher education is one of the major agents in the definition and development of American society. It holds the banner of reason in the creation and management of public policy, and any standard bearer of such importance should not be muddled or mute. If higher education cannot be clear about its own identity, then how can it serve the nation in this role? Both Alice and the institution carry the weight of nations on their shoulders.

While there are many ways to examine and answer questions of personal identity, in this book, I examine those simplicities known as *values* for enlightenment, identity boiled down to its essences, Who are you? answered in twenty-five words or less. *The New York Times* ("Taken at Their Word," 1994) asked some celebrities to perform the same exercise. They provided one-word labels for themselves. Most of the answers seemed to be values statements about the respondents. David Dinkins said that he was "caring"; Eileen Ford said that she was "busy"; Norman Mailer said that he was "improvisational"; and quite predictably, Eartha Kitt said that she was "earthy." Her name had become her essence, her value.

The Nature of Values

Values are summaries of our beliefs—catchphrases that explain who we are. They are the backbone of our behaviors, the great simplicities that spring from the deepest wells of our existence (Wiggins, 1991). Values emerge from our histories, they represent us in the present, and they guide us toward the future. Values are not the same as faith, but they are not incompatible with it either. They emanate from the world's great religious, political, and economic traditions, and the important values—capital-letter VALUES—have been around so long that they are seldom articulated or questioned. Values are not mere passion either, although they are compelled by passion. Nor are they just facts or attitudes or behaviors, but they are related to each of those things. Values synthesize our experiences; they affect how we view things and people. They *will* be acted upon—whether we recognize them or not.

Some values are conscious, like personal mission statements, but many lie beneath the surface of our knowing. We make values-related choices all the time, for example, when we pick dinner from the menu or a new car from the lot. Most of the time, we do not think about our values and even more often, we do not explore the relationships among the values that guide our decisions.

Values can seem to be abstract or real, subjective or objective, ends or means, moral or material, and sometimes all of the above. Usually, values connote a real relationship between subjects and objects that gives meaning to both. What we do and who we are are related notions. For example, academic freedom is one of the most important values of higher education, but people invoke this value only when they are concerned about real people and issues. They might ask what this freedom means; in other words, it is freedom for *who* to do *what*? Why do professors need special freedom to

voice their opinions? Why should society protect academic freedom as much as it protects the right to vote? The real referents
bring values down to earth, where they concern actual people and
their behaviors.

A Values Dilemma

Consider the following dilemma. You are the president of a religiously affiliated liberal arts college in southern Ohio. You are an
ordained minister as well as president. You marched with Dr. King
in Alabama and were jailed because of your belief in integration.
Last week, you expelled an African American fraternity from campus for branding initiates despite the prohibition of hazing on
campus. African American students are sitting in the halls outside
your office protesting this decision and demanding separate residential facilities, social organizations, and an African American
studies program on campus; they insist that you just cannot understand their situation. They have been joined by gay students,
women students, Hispanics, and Asians who want their own interests represented on campus. The board president wants you to do
anything that will keep the students quiet, because enrollment is
down and any negative publicity could imperil the survival of your
college. The church refuses to ordain women, it has ordained only
a handful of African Americans, and it considers homosexuality to
be an unnatural lifestyle. What do you do to resolve the immediate and long-term situations and even more important, how do you
go about deciding what to do as president?

This scenario is laden with values, as all human scenarios are.
This one is filled with concerns about justice, truth, freedom,
equality, and community, as well as the relationship of these values
to the service of an institution. Conflicts among these values affect
everything the president would do to resolve the situation. By understanding the nature and priority of these values and their conflicts, you, the president should be able to make a better decision.
You will know what is important and what is not, what is in conflict
and what is in congruence with your thinking. Some students will
picket outside your office no matter what you do, because decisions
involving values will never please all parties. Reading this book will
protect nobody's job, but it might preserve your integrity as an ed-

ucator and administrator, and you might be able to sleep better at night, knowing that you have helped your institution serve in the best way possible.

The Illusion of Values Neutrality

Values-laden decisions are part of the daily life of every trustee, administrator, and professor in the academy. Understanding a network of values will help each and every one of these parties do better work. It is easy but wrong to join those who think they answer the dilemmas of the academy by refusing to consider the values inherent in them. These people present measured but monotoned arguments about Truth and the need to be impersonal and impartial while seeking or teaching it. The value of the university rests in its values neutrality. All interests are equally shunned.

Values neutrality is impossible. A person or institution that refuses to transmit one set of values is substituting another in its place. Values neutrality is a values stance as much as any other. No enterprise can be fully objective or values neutral, no matter how scientific its nature. Science is not just a set of ideas supported by abstract equations; it is as much or more a set of hunches supported by observations. Both the observer and the observed are part of any phenomenon; method and matter interact. Investigating an object changes it, so neutrality is a scientific impossibility, despite its desirable role in the scientific process. Yet the advocates of neutrality still have many followers, and their popularized version of science persists. But even if neutrality were factually verifiable, its advocates would still be preaching values as much as any other values advocates in the academy. Neutrality stands somewhere in line with the other values of higher education, not above them.

Determining Values from the Inside Out

The academy must think about the values that guide what it does. The study of values should take place inside the halls of ivy more often than it occurs inside the offices of politicians, business people, and others who complain about the waywardness of universities and colleges.

At one time, the study of values was part of the daily life of the academy and the society that sustained it. On the gateway to Ohio University are some words taken from the Northwest Ordinance of 1787, the law that established the university and assured the spread of public higher education into the frontier: "Religion, morality, and knowledge being necessary to good government and the happiness of mankind, schools and the means of education shall forever be encouraged." Every day, students walk past the words that are sculpted on this gateway, but in recent years, few may have pondered their meaning.

The consideration of values was more familiar than foreign in the colonial college. That college was knotted up in the eternal verities of Truth, Beauty, and Good. In the antebellum period, American college presidents were moral philosophers and members of the clergy. They taught and preached that the Truth of God ruled the truths of physical science. The social sciences emerged from this consideration of philosophy, not apart from it. The university was a handmaiden of the church, and scholarship was a service to God. Even in this century, Robert Hutchins, president of the University of Chicago and a champion of classical learning, looked for first principles to guide higher education, principles that were rooted in theology.

For much of this century, however, we have held radically different opinions. The value of the good life has become more important than the value of a life of good. Students dismiss the need to develop a meaningful philosophy of life, and few colleges advertise their impact on the moral development of students; instead, they boast about their impact on future earnings. That is not something to be ignored, but higher education is supposed to improve the human condition in more than economic ways. It must serve a higher purpose.

The treatment of diverse groups in society has confounded values cohesion. The protest movements of the 1960s, 1970s, and 1980s made many people sensitive to everyone else's cause: civil rights, student rights, women's rights, gay rights, and even the rights of animals. However, what was first a molecular movement has become a general scurrying around of unrelated atoms. Everyone is doing a "[*fill in here*] thing; you wouldn't understand." For some people, multiculturalism means that no shared values are defensible; for others it means a chance to assert the supremacy of their own values. For most, multiculturalism means increased sensitivity to people they had not thought about before and a concomitant uncertainty about their own values. The values of the Judeo-Christian European American heritage are no longer the glue of society; they are allegedly one more symptom of its decay. Nobody can be trusted to put things back together again, so why try?

Another indicator of a please-all, help-nobody-in-particular mentality has been found in the expansion of American institutions during the past thirty years. During the 1970s and 1980s, single-purpose businesses were taken over by multi-interest corporations. Research and development were cut; protection through diversification was the path to success. In higher education, the gradual rise of the multiversity during the 1960s was coupled with an explosion in the number of comprehensive community colleges. In the 1970s and 1980s, liberal arts colleges followed the example of both these institutions by offering such things as weekend executive MBA programs. They argued that they had to change the curriculum so they could survive the downturn of traditional student numbers. Maybe so, but the founders of these colleges would have been shocked. "All things to all people" was the shared slogan of higher education and of the business conglomerate up through the 1980s.

Today, business is moving back to doing a few things instead of everything. Perhaps it has discovered the wisdom in the comment that an institution that tries to do everything does nothing particularly well. The academy might learn something from that wisdom. Although most higher education institutions are still trying to diversify their programs and purposes, they should be aware that the public views them as representing nothing more than the current values of the economic and political marketplaces. The academy has come to be viewed as politically correct or morally vapid by critics from the right *and* left of the American political continuum.

This leads us back to values, to the need to see the academy as a secular church that stands for more than material success. The academy is supposed to transmute knowledge into wisdom, and wisdom involves values as well as facts. John Brubacher (1976) says that wisdom emerges from knowledge when what is true about the nature of things is reshaped to human need and oriented to human hope. Some viewpoints are better than others, and the best viewpoints must be used by the academy to help humankind.

You should close this book with a greater understanding of these viewpoints, and of the values issues and service potential of the academy. However, you will also conclude that no one can easily answer the identity question that the Caterpillars have presented to higher education: Who *are* you?

This book provides a different looking-glass, one the academy can use in answering questions about its identity and its values— not a looking-glass with perfect reflection but one with enough lenses to refract the service of the academy in several different ways. While any list of values distorts the very image it attempts to define, it still provides a starting point—a way to begin a necessary discussion about the identity of the academy. So let us begin at our beginning.

Part One

Values We Prize

Some thirty years ago, Raths, Harmin, and Simon (1966) wrote that there were three stages in the valuing process: choosing values, prizing them, and acting on them. The first part of this book concerns the choosing and prizing of seven values—values that together constitute the heritage and the hope of the democratic academy.

Chapter Two

Service: The Value of Altruism

The academy must serve. This is its compact with society. *How* the academy serves and *whom* it serves can be debated, but not the notion *that* it serves (or at least that it should try to do so). This is its fundamental purpose. The institution exists because the public needs its services, and faculty and administrators are measured by their services to students and society (Martin, 1977b).

Serving the public fulfills the public trust. It makes the academy moral instead of just material, because ethical behavior can be described as behavior that is not motivated by self-interest. Ethical behavior serves others or some ideal. Thus, the academy that tries to serve *altruistically* can be judged on moral terms, as well as on political and economic ones.

Service is conceived here as primarily selfless in nature, but it is easy to recognize that the boundaries between self*ishness* and self*lessness* are sometimes fuzzy. The altruistic service in this chapter differs from kindred forms that are described in the chapters on capitalism and spirituality. Here the focus is on the benefit of service to others. Capitalistic altruism looks more like barter; good service helps retain customers. Spiritual altruism involves sacrifice—generosity that can hurt the generous. The main point here is simply that the academy must serve a higher purpose than its own survival.

The key points in this discussion are as follows. First, the functions of teaching, research, and service serve a larger purpose than the perpetuation of the academy and academicians. Second, the goal of academic service is an applied ideal of human betterment, not some abstract ideal of ultimate Truth. Third, academic values and their concomitant rights take their meaning from the responsibilities of academic service. Fourth, even though academic service should be fundamentally altruistic, it is not purely selfless in nature. Fifth, selfless service is not just an obligation of faculty, it is required of all the members of the academy. Sixth, service extends beyond simple duty. The final point in the chapter is that service fulfilled is synergetic.

Buttering Someone Else's Bread

Teaching, research, and service functions are the means of academic service, not its ends. Therefore, teaching, research, and service must be understood and evaluated in terms of their social benefit (Martin, 1977b). Unfortunately, many laypeople have come to view teaching, research, and some forms of service as functions that benefit academicians more than others. Some academicians muddle things further by declaring that teaching, research, and service functions are ends unto themselves. They are valuable because they do not benefit anyone in particular.

Legislators and the laity are angry at higher education because it has violated the public trust. An exposé such as *ProfScam* (Sykes, 1988) affirms the popular suspicion that all public servants, including academicians, have been buttering their own bread instead of serving it to others. The charge is not new; it is as old as Adam Smith's *Wealth of Nations* (Smith,[1776] 1986), in which he wrote that professors wanted to teach as little as possible. Today, a popular perception has professors desiring to be researchers only because research gets them promoted faster and paid more. Research provides professors with book royalties, consulting appointments, and best of all, graduate assistants to perform the onerous chores of teaching. These types of professors are most successful when they do not serve their students, but even if they perform a few truly charitable services, this just seems to gild their corruption. Charles Sykes (1988) argues that all professors have thus been able to protect their own status and independence. While cheating the public and employers, they pollute the intellectual inheritance of society.

Some academicians do not understand what the tumult is about. They are irritated by challenges to their "sacred" values of academic freedom, tenure, and faculty control of the curriculum (Martin, 1977a). They insist that the functions of the academy—especially research—are good precisely because they do not have any obvious use to any specific person or group. If their experiments lead to unhappy consequences, then the fault lies not with themselves but with the corporate and public officials who apply this knowledge in unfortunate ways. Professors serve something higher; they serve Truth.

Such professors would like to excise any notion that they serve ordinary men and women. The end of their research is pure and above application. Their teaching boosts the powers of the mind. Smart students will understand what these professors are saying, but their lectures and deeds are beyond the ken of common minds. Such puffery turns laypeople on to books like *ProfScam* and turns them off at the polls when they are asked to support public higher education. It would be better—and more accurate—to assure the laity that academic truths, like most other truths, shall set them free, even if we cannot say just when and how that is going to happen.

For the Betterment of Humanity

The idea of serving Truth is popular and important, but it is not sustainable without human referents, that is, real people who are bettered by knowing academic truths. The end of academic service is neither the survival of the academy nor the glorification of an abstract ideal of Truth. It is somewhere in between those two extremes, serving an *applied* ideal of the public good.

The service of the academy is directed toward the betterment of all humanity, at least eventually. It is not proscribed by any particular local, state, or national boundaries. Academic service is bigger than that, even though a broad conception of the public good is unacceptable to some sponsors of higher education. Recent history provides many examples of professors who "served" their society by yielding too easily to political and economic dictates. These professors violated the value of academic service. They had an underdeveloped sense of *whom* the academy serves. It does not serve a state; it serves humanity. It does not serve an abstract truth; it serves humanity. Throughout the history of higher education, students, patrons, states, and nations have wanted to own the products of academic service. University research has been used to serve national policy. Weapons research has enhanced the standing of many "top 100" research universities. Colleges have socialized students in keeping with popular politics. During the 1950s, many faculty signed loyalty oaths and questioned the patriotism of those who did not. Today, right-wing and left-wing speakers are disinvited from the podia of public institutions, ostensibly because their remarks might incite violent reactions.

Professors of value balk when sponsors oppose academic values such as truth and freedom, not as ends in themselves but as values related to the betterment of humanity. They frame their argument for such rights as academic freedom in moral as well as epistemological terms, in terms that relate to serving the public interest. These faculty know that society relies on higher education as the principal agency for gaining new knowledge that increases our understanding of the world and improves the human condition.

Paul Goodman (1964) writes that higher education must transcend any regional and national concerns so that it can educate to a universal and potential culture. He says that the culture of the academy is inevitably foreign, no matter where the institution is situated. Ultimately, it was this foreignness, this humanism, that made a university, not some temporal location or focus. Goodman might have been pleased by the response of Frederick Eby when he was asked, "To whom does the University of Texas belong?" Professor Eby answered, "To the world of scholarship" (Sanchez, 1966).

All academic values, rights, and responsibilities are based on the value of service to humankind. Faculty hold on to the values of freedom and truth in order to serve, but they also willingly give up some professional freedoms in order to serve.

Freedom to Serve

Some freedoms are restricted in research and teaching to preserve altruistic service. For example, the 1940 "Principles on Academic

Freedom" of the American Association of University Professors (AAUP) states that the professor is not free to pursue research for pecuniary return; he or she must negotiate this activity with the university. The professor with tenure is guaranteed a sufficient degree of economic security as well as the freedom to do research. More would seem selfish, and this charge of selfishness more than any other seems to have led the recent condemnation of the research accounting at Stanford and other institutions. The nature of the research is less important to the public than the entrepreneurial motives of these universities. They have failed the public criterion of selfless service through research, and more public control will be placed on research at all American universities as a consequence.

Teaching freedoms can be restricted, too, in order to serve the public better. The 1940 AAUP Principles do not allow professors to teach controversial material that is not germane to the subject. *Germane* is the most important term, since the AAUP has stated that it does not want to reduce controversy in the classroom. Extraneous material does not serve students. Professors accept other limitations to their teaching as well. While many professors of English would like to teach another course on Shakespeare instead of composition, they yield their personal interests to serve students better. The same rule affects the entire curriculum; the proponents of the classic liberal arts do not oppose the teaching of new subjects, because they understand that society needs applied science as much as Greek.

The specific service functions of faculty must also meet this general obligation of selflessness. However, the rights of faculty to perform these functions have not been explored. The academic rights of service functions should be determined by their scholarly or administrative nature. This indicates whether the faculty serve the society-at-large through their scholarship or a particular agency through other skills or through the status of their positions in the academy.

When professors serve incorporated agencies instead of their scholarship, they do not represent the common good but an agency with specific political or economic power. This seems obvious in regard to profit-making agencies, but it is equally true when the professor or administrator represents a university, a professional association, or a social service enterprise. The major criterion of service activities is their selflessness, meaning here the absence of personal, economic, or political advantage.

Impure Altruists

Some of the concerns about academic service are exacerbated by the fact that professors usually serve themselves when they serve others. All people have two imperatives, to preserve themselves and their species. A primal dilemma is deciding when one is more important than the other (Kolb, 1984). Clarifying the nature of this decision has kept many philosophers employed, but the choice is seldom discrete for academicians. The livelihood of professors and other public servants is based on their service to others, so altruistic service boosts their economic as well as enlightened self-interest. Professors are not purely altruistic, but then again, few people are. *Pure* altruism is possible on a small scale, over the short term, in certain circumstances, and within small, intimate groups. Anyone who promises better should be distrusted, and any large group professing better should have policies, rules, and regulations that restrain its nascent egoism (Hardin, 1977).

It should be noted that there is a gentler conception of the self-service of altruists. The homily "It is better to give than to receive" has the correspondent truth that the giver gets back as much as he or she gives. This includes praise and the feeling of being useful, but something far more essential can be tapped as well—an apprehension of the deepest values of life.

The only way to find out whether individual professors are trying to help themselves or society is by asking them about their service priorities. Of course, some of these professors might not know what their priorities are, or they might not reveal their priorities even if they do. Who is asking? remains the measure of self-revelation. The professors who do not know their values should read this book. Those who do might trust the questioners after they converse about academic values; this book serves those professors, too. But all groups should understand that service priorities do not have to exclude the professors or others. If the goal of a person's activity is *primarily* selfless, then the service is primarily altruistic. If not, then public suspicion of any public "servant" seems justified.

Consider the following case. Dr. Jones is a professor of geology at a large university in the United States. The university gives him a laboratory, and it pays for the services of a graduate assistant. Research grants pay for laboratory equipment, two more assistants, and the salary of someone to teach Dr. Jones's regular courses. A petroleum company gives him $50,000 a year for consulting services. Dr. Jones earns additional income from an oil production process that he developed in his laboratory at the university. He is going on sabbatical leave next semester, supplementing his salary with a fellowship. So, the question could be posed, What does Professor Jones do for a living?

He *serves*, or at least he is supposed to. All professors are supposed to serve; it is their most important value. Does Professor Jones serve? He has different opportunities from most professors but the same obligation to serve. Even though he operates on a different economic plane, his acts must be judged on the same values plane as other professors.

Service for Status?

All faculty have a fundamental obligation to serve beyond themselves, to sacrifice some personal gains for the benefits of others. In return, they are granted tenure if their service is deemed worthy; they get a concomitant income, and they receive the rights and privileges of professional status.

The original writings of the AAUP declared that tenure protects the service of the professor against the power of his or her employer. Through tenure, the university acknowledges that the professor's major responsibility is to society as a whole and not to any particular board of trustees. A "modest" income was to be associated with tenure to protect the professor from pecuniary interests. To gain more would be unseemly as well as unethical. Professors should maintain the personae of poor but moral scholars, bicycling through town with their gowns flapping dangerously near the spokes. Wheeling the family Lexus into the parking lot destroys the purity of this picture.

Even those faculty who do not earn as much as Professor Jones gain social status because of their occupation. They are elevated above bankers, used car dealers, and merchants. They are *professors* so, therefore, they must be treated as *professionals*.

While few people can define what a profession *is,* they know that it is *not* supposed to be a business, a science, or a racket (Becker, 1956). It is more dignified than those other occupations, and as a result virtually every field of endeavor seems to seek the dignity of professional status. However, only four great professions have stood the test of time—law, medicine, ministry, and university teaching—and only a few others might be accepted among the ranks of the true professions, even though hundreds of near-professions are clawing for this status (Etzioni, 1969).

Most definitions of a profession measure an aspiring occupation against several criteria. The criteria usually include expert knowledge, standards of practice, a private language, training schools, sanctions, and an altruistic mission. The central characteristic in this chapter is the altruistic mission or *service orientation,* which is to attend to the needs of individuals or collectives with competent performance and the interests of society in mind (Young, 1987). True professionals use their technical expertise to fulfill their social commitment. While it can be debated how much any of the three primary academic functions involves the other qualities of a profession, teaching, research, and service demand this service orientation from faculty.

Lest We Forget the Administrators

Professional status is given automatically to faculty, and administrators have reaped some of its rewards as well. Some dignity is attached to working in a college because of its service to society. Perhaps that is one reason why college presidents accept less pay than their counterparts in private enterprise; they enjoy respect for their service. However, *some* professional status is not enough for some administrators. They seek the full-fledged professional recognition that is accorded to faculty. For example, student affairs administration has been classified as a near-profession by several authors in that field (for example, Wrenn and Darley, 1949; Stamatakos, 1981), but many student affairs administrators want faculty to treat them with full respect, as professionals who educate students instead of as adjuncts to the classroom mission. They argue that they deserve greater recognition because serving the student is the central focus of their efforts. Thus, if their services are perceived as ancillary, then too are student interests ancillary to the private interests of professors. While that argument might not be sufficient to gain the laurels of full professional recognition, its fundamental call for status is based on the criterion of service.

This service mission should apply to all administrators, because the etymology of "administer" is *ad-ministrare*, meaning "to serve." The purpose of all administrative work *is* service, whether it is in student affairs, business affairs, or academic affairs. However, administrative service is aimed at specific institutions first instead of the applied ideal of general human betterment. This aim keeps administrators from enjoying the same professional protections, especially tenure, as faculty (Farago, 1981).

Ad-ministry is service, however, and it affects all aspects of the institution, including the educational mission. Continuing with the example of student affairs, these functions are also known as student services that include financial aid, placement, student activities, residential life, admissions, and other functions. There are many different services, but what holds them together is a philosophy of educational service. This philosophy is called the "student personnel point of view" (American Council on Education, [1937] 1986), and it holds that college students are more than minds, they are whole human beings. Therefore, students must be educated inside and outside the classroom about the issues of life. The academy must help them link thought with actions for the benefit of the greater society.

Most faculty, trustees, and other administrators do not know about this point of view, and admittedly some would not care if they did. However, it provides an interpretation of education broader than one restricted to classroom functions or to noncurricular activities. The student personnel point of view deserves a fair hearing, and such a hearing might advance both the status of student affairs and the service of the entire academy.

Dharma, Seva, and Scholarship

On a winter morning stuck in the traffic outside of Erie, Pennsylvania, the voice of Baba Ram Dass came through the speaker in this writer's car. Ram Dass was promoting his book *How Can I Help?* on a talk show. He talked about two different types of service, *dharma* and *seva*. In Hinduism and Buddhism, dharma represents religious law and truth. Dharma is duty, a basic but limited conception of service. Seva, or *sva dharma,* is a personally fulfilled sense of service. Perhaps volunteerism is the better word, but the term *seva* refers to service that transcends a person's minimal duty to society.

The trucks were stopped on Interstate 90, then they started moving slowly, then a little faster, and Ram Dass's voice faded away. However, some people took longer to get back home because they stopped to check on others stranded along the side of the road. Was that their duty or a voluntary act, dharma or seva?

Most members of the academy think of their jobs as service, but they restrict the ways they help students, colleagues, and the general public to the obligations of duty, to the minimum that is needed to fulfill their legal contracts with their employers. This is dharma-service. It holds self-interest within it. Some might call it a legal approach to service rather than a truly ethical one. Legal approaches consist of minimal behaviors to protect people, while ethical ones embrace a higher level of morality than the law requires. Another definition is that ethical behaviors are those in which the actor is not motivated by self-interest but by pure altruism (Farago, 1981). A minimalist, legal, dharma approach to academic work has caused some problems with the public. Academics have not earned the public's respect, because they have not done more than the obvious to serve. Society expects the highest ethical behavior from certain persons who have been entrusted with the public interest. "The amoral person, who obeys only the law but nothing more, may never be convicted, but will also never gain the trust and respect of the community" (Chambers, 1981, p. 4).

In tenure, accreditation, and even promotion decisions, professors and institutions are judged by the numbers of their accomplishments rather than by the quality of service inherent in such things. These forms of validation certify the ends but not the means and motives of accomplishment. Thus, they do not and they cannot be judged fully as service. Only the individual can judge the motive and method and come to a decision beyond Ahab's, that his ends were sane, his means and motive mad. Or even minimal.

Academics must want to serve and must know how. They need a full conceptualization of academic service in order to transcend its minimal obligations.

A way of conceptualizing a full range of academic service is found in Ernest Boyer's (1990) *Scholarship Reconsidered,* in which Boyer draws a continuum of scholarship from discovery through integration to application and, finally, to teaching. Any pause in the middle of the scholarship continuum is convenient for professors who might research more than they teach, but a functional pause cannot be accompanied by conceptual myopia. The functions of scholarship need to be applied for human betterment, otherwise the altruistic value of the academy is unfulfilled. Discovery must contribute to human knowledge. Integration gives meaning to discoveries; it renders intellect wise. Application moves the scholar toward two questions: How can knowledge be reasonably applied to consequential problems? and How can it be helpful to individuals as well as institutions? Teaching involves the learner in these discoveries, meaning-makings, and applications. Teaching is a form of application scholarship directed toward a student population.

Unfortunately, the vision of application service, or seva-service, has all but disappeared from some of the functions of the academy and, as a result, higher education has been criticized for not fulfilling its service mission. Science is one example. The bastion of rationalist research has been criticized by common folk, sometimes legitimately and at other times from a serious lack of understanding, but since the mid-1970s, people have stopped looking at science as an unmixed blessing (Bok, 1982). They have questioned its uses. In recent years, scientists have controlled the choices of their research methods to make their experiments safer for their subjects, but they have spent less time considering the outcomes of those experiments. Laypeople ask why the creators of nuclear fission do not seem to care about its military implications. Just what is a *smart* bomb anyway? The results of scientific research will be applied, and scientists bear some obligation for determining how that will happen. Public service science would be good for the society and the academy. It would restore its intellectual excitement and fun, coupled with the feeling of involvement in a humane and socially beneficial enterprise (Feld, 1975).

Even teaching has not seva-served. Throughout the history of higher education, faculty have been responsible for serving students through their teaching. This was sometimes measured immediately. In the ancient University of Bologna, faculty were paid after every lecture. Students did not pay for teaching that did not meet their standards. Today, few faculty would accept that method of salary distribution even though it is one measure of the effectiveness of their service to students. The faculty would argue, and rightly, that student service through teaching cannot be judged immediately. It is measured long-term by many different yardsticks. This is a seva conception of teaching, and it is manifested through the direct impact of the professor's teachings and through the inculcation of an attitude of service among students.

Perhaps in some former day in America, professors made an impact on their nation through their teaching, but today most lecturers do not try to reach and change society as much as to affirm its political and economic structures. Our contemporary leaders of social change have not been teaching faculty (Boyer, 1990). Instead, these leaders have come from the clergy, just as the first presidents of American higher education emerged from that profession. Those presidents were the most important moral philosophers of their day. They wanted to prepare their students for community leadership and good citizenship. Educational leaders such as Thomas Jefferson in the early nineteenth century and John Dewey in the early twentieth century reinforced the importance of educating students to be informed and active citizens.

Today's faculty seem more quiet, perhaps because they are too close to their own histories. The last thirty years have cast different light and shadows on the value of social service. During the early 1960s, activism was a positive social noun, and service wore a smile. America was on the edge of the new frontier, and baby boomers starting into college would lead us into it. In the late 1960s and early 1970s, social service had an angrier visage. Many students said that the academy had to disrupt society to serve it. Then, through the late 1970s and 1980s, service disappeared from the face of American higher education. Students reported that they were no longer interested in developing a meaningful philosophy of life. Like the founder of Mary Kay Cosmetics, they wanted the money, honey. A memorable cartoon shows Don Quixote, the student of the 1960s, tilting at a windmill with broken-down blades. Next to him is Don Quixote of the 1980s, a student grabbing at huge dollar bills that replace the blades. Students wanted the good life even though they suspected they were buying first-class tickets on America the Titanic (Levine, 1980). Hung over from the boozy expansionist days of the 1960s and 1970s and facing declining enrollments during the 1980s, academies attended to public approval ratings instead of social issues such as inequity. They had to pay for the residence halls and classrooms they had built for the baby boomers. Already stung by some activities that ventured into social reform instead of social criticism, they accepted silently the status *quo* for the *quid* of financial support. Some faculty and administrators even found comfort in classifying their students as selfish. It meant that they did not have to think about seva-service themselves.

The Times, They Are A'Changing?

The spirit of the early 1960s is hovering overhead, getting ready to land. "Altruism Is in Style" was a headline in *U.S. News and World Report* (1994). The article goes on to say, "Self-absorption is passé as this generation of undergraduates, particularly at the national liberal arts colleges, reaches out to the world beyond the campus" (p. 25). Students are reporting different goals. "Being well-off financially" has dropped for the fifth straight year, and developing "a meaningful philosophy of life" has risen over the same period of time. Students are going into the streets, but this time to serve the homeless and not to throw rocks at National Guard troops.

The higher education reform movement of the mid-1980s extolled service-learning for students. Some reports recommended that students take a mandatory course in community service (for example, Bell, 1986). The psychological benefits were abundant. Service activities increased empathy and self-esteem and altruism in students. They helped students plan careers, become motivated, and accept their duty to become responsible, engaged adults. In *College: The Undergraduate Experience,* Boyer (1987) concluded the section on service learning with this reference from Woodrow Wilson: "It is not learning, but the spirit of service that will give college a place in the public annals of the nation." Teaching, as seva-service, must invoke this spirit.

One additional component of service learning is important to mention—the *learning* philosophy behind the activities. It is a seva-philosophy. While it is important to talk about teaching, research, and service activities as service functions, they are based on the role of the academy-as-expert. Service-learning can remove the guise of expertise and replace it with a spirit of mutuality (Berte and O'Neil, 1977). Later in this book, this spirit will be evoked within the value of community. Service-learning enables the faculty member, the administrator, and the institution to share in the learning process. The process is more dynamic because it enables the academy to grow as much as the agencies or individuals being served. This reflects the principle that roles disappear in truly selfless service. Altruism is the antithesis of egoism. There is no perception of giver and receiver; instead, there is an engagement in the process of service rather than a measurement of the size of gifts, a spirit of grace merely to have the opportunity to serve: "We've simply remembered who we all really are behind the roles" (Dass and Gorman, 1991, p. 140). The whole is more, a celebration of the synergy and not the status of the parts.

Conclusion

Most of the preceding discussion seems obvious. The academy must *serve* if it is to fulfill its value to humanity. But some professors have not met the full demands of their public trust. They have made eloquent arguments about their need to research and to teach, but they have not satisfied the public that these activities give back as good as they get. H. M. Jones (1967) has stated that elitist faculty have made an incoherent argument to an egalitarian populace about their needs and interests. They need to make their case intelligible to the "common man," that professors have been trained to do a job that helps. In the state of Ohio, it is obvious that this case has not been made. In 1992, higher education received 12 percent of the funds of that state, but it absorbed 35 percent of the cuts in that year's budget. Ohio universities were told that they did not serve the people as much as other institutions in the state.

These charges are familiar, and their financial consequences limit the academy's ability to teach and research and apply scholarship. It must convince the public, but first itself, that more can be done to serve. The academy must research and teach and serve for the betterment of humankind, and it must transcend minimal service in its arguments and deeds. By moving all of its activities toward the application of scholarship, the academy seva-serves. It is no longer fractured by its expertise. Roles disappear, and synergy appears. The people within the academy are connected with those outside. The functions of the academy become a whole, welded together by the value of selfless service.

| **Truth: Not an End in Itself**

Truth is automatically included among the essential values of higher education, no matter how this value is defined. Almost every member of the academy believes that higher education must find and teach what is true. Determining what is true, and from that determining what is Truth, is a subject of greater controversy.

Truth stands next to beauty and good as one of Plato's three great virtues. Truth might stand out from the other two virtues, because it refers to abstractions more than to tangible things. A thing of beauty might be a joy forever, and a good man might be hard to find, but an idea has never been seen, felt, or tasted. Despite this abstractness, the search for truth is the ruling rationale for the academy. "Veritas" is the motto of Harvard, "Lux et Veritas," the motto of Yale. In the cathedral of learning, we like to believe that we all kneel at the altar of truth.

Academic truth has come to differ from spiritual truth—the subject of a subsequent chapter—and no holy trinity will be mentioned here. There is, however, a secular trinity of truths, otherwise known as rationalism, empiricism, and pragmatism. The first is the oldest of the three, embracing the mind as the most important characteristic of humanity and ideas as the most important creations in an otherwise sensate world. Empiricism upholds faithfulness to facts. Truth is discovered through the senses; the mind cannot be trusted all by itself. The final incarnation is the most American. Pragmatism sees truth as an outcome of experience. I will describe these three forms of truth later in this chapter, but most academics endorse one or more of them.

Middle-Sized Truth

In the daily devotionals of academic life, truth looks like a middle-sized value. Truth can seem mighty in its abstraction, but its demands are usually down to earth. An administrator chooses between her loyalty to the institution and her pledge to be an honest accountant. A researcher decides whether to fudge his findings or face the disappointments of another failed experiment. A professor selects what to teach. In these instances and most others, the academy's value of truth might foster important decisions, but it is truth spelled with a little "t," not a big "T." The latter spelling makes Truth a spiritual value instead of an educational one (Smith, 1970).

It takes scrupulousness, doubt, and tolerance to find little truths and perhaps not much more than that. Lower-case virtues fit lower-case aspirations. For example, Montaigne abandoned his search for absolute truth and settled for the smaller, personal traits of doubt and tolerance. Yet the lower-case virtues can yield many substantial truths to be contemplated and enjoyed in their own right. If the reader wants to turn such discoveries into the adoration of some greater, universal Truth, that is fine. However, such reverence is not necessary to get through this chapter.

Truth involves process and product, the way and the light. The way includes reason and observation. Reason creates theories, and observation tests them. The light is called knowledge, which must be differentiated from mere opinion. At its best, knowledge is fact. At a minimum, it is theory supported as much as possible by facts. Its home is the curriculum. Summing process and product yields epistemology, the study of knowledge. The rest of this chapter involves this study, by taking the reader on a journey through various interpretations of truth in the academy.

I will discuss the following points in this chapter. First, the academy is concerned mostly with changing, contextual, middle-sized truths. Second, different conceptions of truth guide different types of colleges and the functions of teaching, research, and service. Third, a pragmatic vision of truth can embrace research and teaching as well as the other service functions of the academy. Fourth, all the service functions of the academy—research, teaching, service—

must be measured by the application of truths to better humanity; and finally, the diversity of truths discovered vitalizes the system of American higher education when it is delivered coherently.

Traveling Toward Truth

Somewhere between Annapolis, Maryland and Washington, D.C., you might come to a crossroad. The directions to nearby colleges are posted on signs in front of you. To the east is St. John's College. To the north is Johns Hopkins University. To the south is Prince George's Community College, and to the west is the University of Maryland at College Park. You are looking for the Academy of Truth, which is located in any direction you might take. Just ask the administrators and faculty at any one of these campuses, and they will tell you that Truth is located there. Being men and women of good will, they might also point out that truth can be found in different forms at other nearby institutions.

When you arrive on campus at any Academy of Truth, you might see that the philosophy department is to the right of you, and straight ahead is chemistry. Go left if you want to find the school of education, and turn around if you want to reach history. But every college, building, and department on this campus is marked with the same label—Truth. The administrators and faculty in every building will tell you that you have come to the right place to find Truth. Being men and women of good will, they might also point out that truth can be found in different forms in other buildings.

The Rationalist College

If you thought that the Academy of Truth could be found at the St. John's campus, then you would be in the vicinity of rationalist truth. In that type of academy, the mind is the key to experience, and the classics form the curriculum. There may be many new things under the sun, but the classics shed more light on the world than most undergraduates can stand.

St. John's is a teaching college that requires its undergraduates to read their set of Great Books. The curriculum is prescribed, just as it was prescribed in the universities of the Middle Ages, with their emphasis on the trivium and the quadrivium, the seven ancient liberal arts. The three ways of understanding truth—grammar, rhetoric, and logic—are still required on the St. John's campus. The 1937 catalogue of St. John's called them, "the three R's, reading, writing, and reckoning . . .[and] it is their integrity and power that still lure us back to the little red school houses where our fathers and grandfathers studied and practiced them" (Shoemaker, 1943, p. 150). Every Great Book in the St. John's curriculum "must be a masterpiece in the liberal arts. It must have that clarity and beauty on its surface which provides an immediate intelligibility and leads the mind of the reader to its interior depths of illumination and understanding" (Shoemaker, 1943, p. 151). Students move from ancient Greek literature through the Middle Ages into the nineteenth- and twentieth-century authors. No matter the dates of their readings, all students are reinforced in the ways of the liberal arts.

Teaching the classics involves both the process and product of rationalist truth. The arts of reading, writing, and reckoning increase the ability of a student to understand and explain the facts of the world. The facts are deduced from general principles that are found in classic texts. Deduction is the first form of logic, and to some people it remains the essence of a university. The purpose of the mind is to find those truths that cohere with reality, not to make up realities. Time determines which truths are made up and which endure. Therefore, the classic texts are the source of eternal truths that help us understand reality and increase our capacity for moral action.

In the rationalist institution, professors choose the curriculum so that students can master concepts and skills. The authority of determining and protecting the truth is invested in the faculty, an investiture that few professors would care to dispute. Lectures transmit information. Socratic dialogues are used to debate information. Testing, grades, and brain power are emphasized in the rationalist university.

The rationalist college is proud to be a small, single-purpose institution instead of a larger, multipurpose conglomerate. Perhaps it is the true *uni*-verse-ity. The president is the leader of the faculty and unafraid to preach the powers of the mind. In this century, the most renowned leader of such an institution was Robert M.

Hutchins. Best known for his presidency at the University of Chicago, Hutchins (with Mortimer Adler) revised substantially the curriculum of that institution and, later, arranged the general publication of a Great Books series. Hutchins (1967) created a syllogism that explains the rationalist college: "Education implies teaching. Teaching implies knowledge. Knowledge is truth. The truth is everywhere the same" (p. 66).

Hutchins railed against the confusion, anti-intellectualism, relativism, and vocationalism of American higher education. He appealed to the traditions of the *Higher Learning in America* for the resolution of all problems. Absolute, higher-order, and metaphysical truth could integrate the curriculum and teachings of the American college.

Hutchins's words echoed those of the ancients—Aristotle, for example—and they are restated today by William Bennett, Alan Bloom, E. D. Hirsch, and others. Bennett (1984) claims that "few [college students] can be said to receive there adequate education in the culture and civilization of which they are members. . . . The fault lies principally with those of us whose business it is to educate students. . . . It is we, the educators [who] have given up the great task of transmitting a culture to its rightful heirs" (p. 1). He calls for strong presidents to make plain the mission of higher education, which is to provide a traditional, liberal arts curriculum so that students become educated persons, regardless of their major fields of study.

Some regard Bennett and his counterparts as fossils, or worse as fascists. At a minimum, these rationalists are deemed naive, because they believe that objective processes can prevail over such base things as senses and emotions and that reason can civilize power and save America from political ruin (Marsden, 1994; Wiggins, 1991). Hutchins received this sort of criticism, too. For example, John Dewey abhorred Hutchins's solutions of intellectual contemplation and great books. Dewey believed that science had advanced truth-seeking beyond the limits that the ancient canon could explain. However, he ignored the fact that many professors in rationalist colleges invoke the findings of modern science and the concepts of modern authors to evaluate the canon that they teach.

The Empirical University

An institution physically near St. John's is light-years away in its conception of academic truth. Johns Hopkins University was established in 1876 as the first true university in America, meaning a research university, one that emulated German institutions and embraced the empirical method of finding truth, inducing general principles from the observed facts of sensory life. Empirical means "under test." Truth is attached to statements that agree directly or indirectly with the facts. There are many facts, so there are many types of truth. The value of any truth varies in proportion to the amount of evidence that supports it.

Some institutions became empirical, and others had empiricism thrust upon them. But Johns Hopkins was born an empirical university. Its first president, Daniel Coit Gilman, had studied in Germany, and under his direction, the university admitted only the best and brightest students to study under the best and brightest faculty. When he was asked how to start a university, Gilman answered simply, "Enlist a great mathematician and a distinguished Grecian; your problem will be solved. Such men can teach in a dwelling house as well as a palace" (Flexner, 1946, p. 91). Gilman spent no money on buildings; those resources were earmarked for faculty salaries. He did not organize the faculty. They were free to teach and research whatever they chose, so long as their colleagues agreed with these choices. Johns Hopkins was the first American university to identify the undergraduate "major" and "minor," even though all undergraduate teaching was viewed as a distraction to its specialized research faculty.

The first Hopkins faculty were renowned scholars, but their teaching abilities could be questioned. Henry Rowland, who built the first real physics laboratory at an American university, was a good example. Some said that Rowland neglected his students, even though one admirer said that being neglected by him was more stimulating and inspiring than the closest supervision of lesser men.

Teaching serves research at Hopkins or any other empirically based university. Empiricists believe that the classical, liberal arts curriculum belongs in schools or in colleges, not in true universities.

The purpose of teaching is to train incoming generations of scholars and scientists for the pursuit of knowledge. Training for other purposes is best done elsewhere.

The supporters of the empirical university consider it to be the best and brightest modern university of truth, but it struggled to reach this level of respect. The first American scholars went to Germany in 1810, but almost a century passed before the research university surpassed the rationalist college as the paragon of academic excellence. Today, a reader has to look hard to find any colleges in the latest annual *Best Colleges* issue of *U.S. News and World Report*. The first reports are about "national universities," and thirty-five of the top fifty of those institutions are listed as Research I Universities in the Carnegie classification system. They award at least fifty Ph.D.'s annually, and they receive at least $40 million in federal support each year, much of it for research. These same institutions dominate the lists of "best departments," such as physics and economics and English. The national liberal arts colleges and their less prominent comrades, the regional liberal arts colleges, can be found toward the back of the issue.

In a commentary about colleges, character, and jazz, Warren Bryan Martin (1982) compares the college to pianist Oscar Peterson and the university to trumpeter Miles Davis. Peterson does not invent music; he interprets it. Martin writes that the college is like that: "It knows its place and it does its job; it is true to itself" (p. 19). The "true" empirical university is like Miles Davis, bent on discovering new modes of expression, sometimes on the outer edge of musical taste.

The empirical university is instrumental, but only in the sense of putting data together, not the musical sense. Its form of reason is inductive and not deductive. It forms principles from collections of facts and calls them probable instead of certain. Two kinds of truths are considered empirical, those that can be verified by experience and those that help analyze experience. The first involve sensory data, while the second involve theories, mathematical formulae, and the like. The first led to pragmatism. The second led to logical positivism.

I will discuss pragmatism later, but positivism has been the primary support of values neutrality in the academy. Positivism holds that all metaphysical, religious, ethical, and poetic concepts are meaningless, because they cannot be verified through science. They are pseudo-concepts that arouse emotion but lack cognitive significance. Subjectivistic, relativistic, and ultimately arbitrary, these pseudo-concepts cannot be validated, only asserted (Sloan, 1980).

Reason is not immune to the influence of emotion; thus, positivism is unimpressed by the methods and goals of the rationalist college. The positivist considers the mind to be the pawn of primordial emotions. Reason is the "computerized instrument for discovering means to emotively determined ends or of . . . masking hidden and conventionally disreputable motives" (Harris, 1970, p. 99).

Many allegedly factual concepts can rest on emotional grounds. What appears to be true often is not. A 1994 *Smithsonian* magazine story carried the banner, "Don't look now—but all those plotters might be hiding under your bed." The author, Robert Wernick, writes about the great American penchant for real and imagined conspiracies. One illustration of this phenomenon is found in Henry Louis Gates, Jr.'s 1996 interview with Louis Farrakhan. Gates found a remarkable similarity between the world-order conspiracy theories of Farrakhan and Pat Robertson. Both believe that a Jewish cabal is running the world and suppressing everyone else. Both believe they are telling the truth when they spout these theories, and both receive standing ovations from their audiences when they share them. Still, not many Black Muslims attend Robertson revivals, and few white evangelicals stop by the South Side to embrace others who share their beliefs.

Emotion can subvert truth in ways that seem less evil. The words *Iwo Jima* inspire memories of a picture of the raising of the flag on Mount Suribachi. Most Americans think this picture was taken while the soldiers were in mortal combat. Actually, it shows the raising of a second flag on Mount Suribachi, done during an impromptu ceremony after the great battle. Apparently, nobody wants to recognize this fact. Karal Marling and John Wetenhall (1993) describe a "vortex of misremembering" in which hearsay and emotion quickly subsumed the truth. "It is an overwhelming reverence for the heroic feeling of the Iwo Jima myth that still renders the *facts* of its birth—to some people at least—irrelevant" (p. A52).

Even in the classroom, it can be difficult to challenge popular myths with facts. For example, Nancy Shoemaker (1993) writes that her older students are convinced that the history of the American West was mostly good, while the younger ones think it was mostly evil. Just as the older students do not want to recognize the human weaknesses of American cowboys, the younger students do not want to learn any unpleasant facts about American Indians. Facts can dispute our comfortable mythologies about people. However, no one should dispute that emotion affects the interpretation of many facts and beliefs. The logical positivist concludes, therefore, that emotion and its major partners—religion and aesthetics— have a distinctly subordinate place in the academy.

The empiricist does not favor the use of the university for social reform. At first, this avoidance was due to the empiricists' faith in science. As precise scientific problems were solved, precise ethical issues would solve themselves. Since World War I, however, logical positivism has moved social and natural science faculty away from social action. These fields have become dominated by a stress on a scientific, objective, and quantitative understanding of research.

Empiricism has shattered the myth that scientific knowledge is fundamentally whole and one. This was the first truth of the rationalist college, this wholeness of knowledge that a university stands for (Conant, 1964). Empiricism has fractured the claim. It has focused on the acquisition of knowledge in many different specialized areas, expanding the possibilities of the *universe*-ity, while minimizing the synthesis of knowledge, the focus of the *uni*-verse-ity. Empirical research has produced many unconnected trivialities, new truths that are atomistic rather than molecular. The new, little truths have yielded few generalizations about one big one. Empiricists have found moss, not metaphysics, under every stone. It might be true that 90 percent of all scientists are alive today, but how many empiricists does it take to match a single Leonardo?

The Pragmatic Institution

Some people would go west to College Park, to the University of Maryland, to find a pragmatic Academy of Truth. Other drivers might head south to Prince George's Community College. The land grant university is the alma mater of the community college, which has in turn been democracy's foremost college during the last forty years. Both institutions constitute the pragmatic American vision, that in matters of truth (and most others as well), action is more important than insight.

Pragmatism is the child of empiricism, and it shares its parent's distrust of thought without concomitant observation. The mind is a verb. Believing is one thing, while knowing is another. William James—one of the parents of pragmatism—said, "True ideas are those that we can assimilate, validate, corroborate, and verify. False ideas are those that we cannot" (cited in Boller, 1980, p. 263).

Today, most people use the word *pragmatic* as a synonym for anything useful. Pragmatic truth is what works. Traditional empiricism might look backward at the causes of ideas, but pragmatism looks forward to their consequences. The origin, logic, and elegance of an idea are secondary to its practical outcomes. An idea is an abstraction, so pragmatists believe that it is more important to ask what concrete difference that idea makes in anyone's life. Pragmatists seek solutions to problems, not just information about them. They assume that people struggle for existence and that only the fit survive. Mind, ideas, and science are instruments evolved to aid in that struggle (Bahm, 1980), and knowledge is its offspring.

Pragmatism offers a counterpoint to antiseptic rationalism and empiricism. It questions the ethics of science that confines itself to means instead of ends. It criticizes inaction, whether that is rooted in the analytical mind or in the discovery of causes. John Dewey saw no boundary between moral science and other science. "It is physical, biological, and historic knowledge voiced in a human context where it will illuminate and guide the activities of men" (cited in Sloan, 1980, p. 224). This perception of the purpose of science fits perfectly with the altruistic mission of the university. The academy serves when truth serves. Truth is not valued because it is intrinsically worthwhile, nor is it ever absolute, because absolutes have no intimate relationship with contexts. Pragmatic researchers are not separate from their problems, nor are pragmatic administrators separated from their situations. While the merit of these assumptions can be questioned intellectually, they summarize the everyday American's vision of "true" higher education. It is useful, changing, and contextual.

Most American colleges have been pragmatic. The frontier colleges lacked financial support and sufficient numbers of students. The students who tried to enroll were unprepared for college-level work, so many colleges enrolled more students in school courses than in undergraduate studies. Remedial education was one of the first programs in American higher education. Also, few students on the American frontier wanted to study Latin or Greek or the classic liberal arts. In that western backwater of Charlottesville, Virginia, Thomas Jefferson established eight professorships: ancient languages, modern languages, mathematics, natural philosophy, natural history, medicine, moral philosophy, and law. The titles sounded traditional, but students in modern languages could study modern geography, students in natural philosophy could learn about hydraulics and mechanics, and students of natural history could study about mineralogy and rural economy. The practical arts were not ignored in the university that Jefferson—the great intellectual, inventor, architect, farmer, and politician—built.

The Land Grant Act of 1862 mortared with public funds the individual brick work of the frontier colleges. American higher education was remade by the Act that validated for the first time the teaching of agriculture and mechanical arts without excluding other scientific and classical studies. Anything useful would be taught and, in some institutions, supported by the federal government.

Pragmatic philosophy has been given credit for the development of the state university, where the curriculum is no longer bound to the liberal arts and participation no longer restricted to intellectuals (Taylor, 1970). The state university is a place where people are taught what they must know in order to live in modern society. There is no conflict between vocational training and liberal education there. The curriculum contains those studies and fosters those experiences that are significant to individual lives and, at the same time, relevant to the needs of society. This does not exclude the classics, but it makes the test of their utility more immediate.

Thus, travelers to the University of Maryland can even find a rationalist college or two and an empirical university on campus, but they should not end their journey at these buildings. Rationalism and empiricism are useful components of the central mission of truth at this institution.

In recent years, the community college has taken on this mission within the cities, suburbs, and counties of America. Like American higher education in general, the community college started out as a junior version of something more traditional. In the early 1960s, two-thirds of its students expected to transfer to four-year colleges, even though only a quarter of them succeeded in this goal. As the college matured, it became the "comprehensive" community college, embracing equally its transfer, vocational, and community-service curricula.

The comprehensive curriculum, whose worth is determined by its utility, is one consequence of the pragmatic philosophy in both the land grant university and the community college. Truth is no longer absolute or even unified knowledge wrapped up in course work, as Mr. Hutchins wished it to be. Knowledge has become relative, experiential, and true only in the pragmatic sense of the term.

Another attribute of the pragmatic philosophy concerns the acceptance of applied research in the academy. Dewey believed that applied science is more truly scientific than its "pure" counterpart. Applied research extends the notion of discovery through use. Applied research has several pragmatic benefits. First, it often is conducted for the goal of human betterment. Second, tangible outcomes reveal the benefits of science to ordinary people better than abstract theorems. They make the production of knowledge an industry in its own right. Finally, the government supports applied research, which then provides greater support for the scientists of pure research (Bahm, 1980). These benefits might affect all science, but they also sustain the priority of the immediate over the eternal, the superficial over the profound, and the commodity over the idea.

Many of the products of science *are* good. New medicines protect against disease, new compounds make better crops, and new appliances increase daily comfort. Pragmatic scientists know these products are good because they are always testing the results of their findings. Empiricists and especially positivists avoid that evaluation. Some of the research of pragmatists will disserve humanity, but their commitment to truth demands that they know how their research affects the world outside the university gates.

Leaving the University of Truth

The road leaving the pragmatic University of Truth does not seem as smooth as the road heading into the rationalist college. The pavement is fractured, and it seems to go in every direction. Induction has been added to the first path deduced. Sense observation has been added to common sense. Action has been added to insight. The roads leading to truth seem to go everywhere—and perhaps nowhere—at the same time.

Conclusion

Every professor and institution must be committed to the search for truth, the ability to declare it well, and the service that this activity provides society. Fulfilling this commitment requires teamwork among the proponents of different versions of truth. Empiricists discover facts that disrupt unified, ultimate meaning. Rationalist academics find the source of this disruption in the classics, and pragmatists see what people will do with the information. All the players are important.

In a fragmented world, unified truth is a Holy Grail, an aspiration more than a reality. It is the cause and the guide of the search more than a certain discovery. The process of the search is at least as important as the product. As Charles Sherrington (1940) notes, "Truth is a value. The quest itself therefore is in a measure its own satisfaction . . . continually approaching, so continually without arrival. The satisfaction [is] eternal" (p. 400).

Scrupulosity, doubt, and tolerance, those middle-sized virtues of this middle-size value, must be practiced every day, even if our hearts are made sore by what we discover and teach. And the impact of our discoveries and teachings cannot be ignored, even if it makes us squirm in our seats.

The lessons of the value of truth seem to be these, conceived by Lawrence LeShan and Henry Margenau (1982) as the restless faith of modern science:

The search for truth is a never ending quest; yet we pledge ourselves to seek it.

All claims to ultimate truth must be tested. Some will be stop signs. "We will ignore them; if they are signposts, we will note them and move on" (p. 70).

Every mystery is a challenge; no subjects or facts are closed to inquiry. The truth must be sought in both the accepted region called science and the "shadowy regions that surround human consciousness, the essence of the mind, including features that are still obscure or occult and mysterious" (p. 71).

Chapter Four

Freedom: Choice with Responsibility

Facts have splintered thought, leaving truth everywhere—and nowhere. Follow the signs in any direction, and the seeker of truth will discover some but not all of it. The seeker of first truths—the foundations for structuring belief—finds instead a theology of pluralism. Many truths are out there, and no comforting unity is hidden behind any of them (Martin, 1982).

Most of the little truths of the academy provide neither big comforts nor big challenges. Any grand truths are too uncertain for empiricists. A latter-day Luther might earn a paragraph in the student newspaper for tacking "Ninety-Five Theses" on the door of today's secular church, but David Letterman would get front-page coverage for pinning the "Ten Top Reasons Why the Biology Department Stinks" on the same door.

Many academics consider it impolite to argue about facts and ideas outside their disciplines, yet all ideas, grand or small, must be held up to scrutiny. Ideas unchallenged become mythology. I cited examples of this in the last chapter: the raising of the flags at Iwo Jima and the settling of the American West. In a conversation with Bill Moyers, E. L. Doctorow (1989) said that unchallenged ideas make people passive, they indoctrinate, and they manipulate. The manipulators of truth must be confronted everywhere in order to drive out falsehoods, and the confronters must be careful in this process to avoid becoming doctrinaire themselves.

Everybody benefits when the academy seems unbalanced in its advocacy of truth, so long as the imbalance appears to be both to the right and left of the mainstream. The advocates of truth cannot substitute any convenient mythology for it, radical or reactionary, no matter how safe that mythology seems to be. Nor can they shrug off arguments about the value of even a factoid, nor bend to threats. Centuries ago, our culture selected the academy as a place where all secular truth could be pursued and shared. To fulfill this obligation to the culture, professors must have the protection and incentive to serve any-sized truth, and their shield and spirit come from the value of freedom.

The basis of the value of academic freedom, like the basis of its companion, truth, is a commitment to service. As John Brubacher (1965) writes, the ethical duty to maintain academic freedom has civil as well as professional dimensions, and the civil dimension is larger and more basic. The 1940 AAUP Principles state that institutions of higher education are conducted for the common good and not to further the interest of either the individual teacher or the institution as a whole. The common good depends upon the free search for truth and its free exposition by parties that serve truth and society selflessly.

Academicians are not only free to serve, they are obliged to do so. Service is the price that society demands for the freedom to pursue truth. Choice cannot be divorced from altruism; freedom requires responsibility. Understanding this interconnection is necessary before the questions of freedom are parsed into who deserves which rights to do what.

Years ago, any questions about individual freedom were answered quickly, sometimes forcefully, and always in favor of the broader community. Socrates drank the hemlock because he had violated community mores with his teaching. Abelard and Galileo were denounced as heretics. The freedom of these men was less important than the rules of their political and religious communities. If they did not like these rules, they could try to change them or leave. If they did not leave, that indicated their choice to obey. This type of freedom gives room for individual conscience and choices, but the community also has a right to expect its members to live by the values they accept through their membership (Estanek, 1995).

Freedom has been constrained covertly as well as overtly in many places. Thomas Jefferson told his faculty at the University of Virginia that they could follow truth wherever it may lead, but he did not hire anyone who disagreed with his political views. At about the same time, anarchist faculty were not employed in the University of Berlin because, the university declared, the state would not respect any university that hired such people. Today, it seems that faculty can say what they think and study what they want. They can turn any number of ways and find a road leading to truth, and wherever they turn, they are liable to bump into fools as well as wise folks.

In the rest of the chapter, I discuss the value of freedom in regard to faculty, administrative, institutional, and student activities. I conclude with a discussion about choice and responsibility. The value of freedom helps determine who deserves the right-of-way in the search for and advocacy of truth.

These are the major points. First, the freedom of faculty is connected to service. Second, faculty must risk the safety of the status quo and actively examine how their knowledge can be applied for the betterment of humanity. Third, the freedoms of faculty to perform "service" functions outside the academy have not been explored. Fourth, administrators protect the freedom of faculty, but their own freedoms are not protected beyond the rights of all citizens. Fifth, the institution must be autonomous enough to protect freedom from external constraints. Sixth, student freedoms warrant more discussion. Finally, shallow conformity disserves the institution more than forthright examinations of academic freedom, institutional autonomy, and academic service.

Faculty Activities

Faculty activities are emphasized in most statements about academic freedom, which is related to the search for and transmission of truth. The search for and transmission of truth emphasizes research and teaching and ignores the last of the triumvirate—service. Such priorities are easy, since service is the least understood and least valued of all faculty activities. However, the emphasis on research and teaching can limit our understanding of freedom and truth. The academic process is incomplete until knowledge has moved from the processes of acquisition through transmission to application, that is, until it has served.

Teaching and Research

Teaching and research are emphasized in the 1940 AAUP Principles. They declare that freedom in research is fundamental to the advancement of truth. Freedom in teaching protects the rights of the teacher in teaching and the student in learning. International documents have a similar focus. For example, the 1988 Lima Declaration defines academic freedom as the individual or collective freedom of faculty in the pursuit, development, and transmission of knowledge. Although the Lima Declaration states that academic freedom is an essential precondition for the administrative and service functions of universities, neither it nor the AAUP document discusses service as a specific professional responsibility.

The oldest function in higher education is teaching, and it could be argued that academic freedom in teaching has been protected in the United States since 1789, when the first amendment to the Constitution was enacted. The freedom to disseminate knowledge through lectures is one form of free speech, and almost all forms of free speech have been protected by our law and courts since the founding of the nation.

Academic freedom in research was imported at the turn of this century, along with the German university. This meant that the German conception of an apolitical, scientific university affected American assumptions of academic freedom. Eventually, graduate research professors came to merit greater rights than undergraduate teachers, and the professors of natural and experimental science merited greater freedoms than their counterparts in the arts, theology, or social sciences. Scientific research was raised above the teaching of subjects that involved the pulpit, people, and power. Professors stopped worrying about the impact of their teaching on student lives. Concern about the consequences of their research was also left to others. It was not as important as the research itself.

Accepting Some Restrictions

As I noted in Chapter Two, faculty have always accepted some restrictions in their research and teaching to preserve the value of service. However, American professors might not appreciate how much their teaching and research could be restricted. When freedom is taken for granted, arguments about the truth are accepted as normal. Many Central and Eastern Europeans, Asians, Latin Americans, and Africans know otherwise. As freedom has brought new ideas into their classrooms, it has exposed the hypocrisy of some of these professors during earlier times. Students in these nations say, "They lied to us when they taught history before the revolution. Why should we believe them now that they teach philosophy?"

Even on this shore, some professors are not safe. An article in *Lingua Franca* (Anton, 1992) describes the assassination of Professor Ioan Culianu by the Romanian secret service. Culianu was a professor of divinity at the University of Chicago, who was killed in a campus bathroom, allegedly because he spoke out on Radio Free Europe and wrote more than thirty articles against the politics in post-Ceausescu Romania. His words burned with the danger around him, even in America, and yet Culianu continued to speak out, to serve freely what he considered to be the truth. His last short story, "The Language of Creation" (1991) is about a box that contains the encoded language of God. The owner tries to use the box against a corrupt political regime, despite the fact that its three former owners have been murdered.

Freedom and Application Scholarship

In some former day in America and in some other societies today, research and teaching threatened convention, making their service less obvious and their protection more imperative. But today, the discoveries and discussions of professors do not change society as much as they affirm its political and economic structures. Some forms of research have brought great money and prestige to faculty and their institutions. These in turn have enhanced the image of those institutions (Astin, 1985). Fine enough, but research that serves must educate as well, and that means it must eventually challenge convention in the classroom as well as in the laboratory.

In *Scholarship Reconsidered*, Ernest Boyer (1990) states that the work of the scholar includes research and teaching, but scholars must also think about the usefulness of knowledge and reflect on the social consequences of their work. In so doing, they can gain understanding of how their own study relates to the world beyond the campus. Boyer calls this form of service *application scholarship*, and he stresses its scholarly character. Application scholarship is tied directly to a scholar's special field of knowledge; it relates to and flows directly from this professional activity, and it requires the rigor and accountability traditionally associated with research activities. Application scholarship includes consultation, technical assistance, policy analysis, and program evaluation. It excludes civic and social projects that are outside the professor's field of inquiry.

When professors are encouraged to accept the rights and obligations of application scholarship, they are encouraged to declare, then implement, the best of the truths that they have uncovered, examined, and discussed in dispassionate ways in the laboratory or classroom. Many are forced to make value judgments about their knowledge. The moral philosopher becomes as important to the university as the physical scientist, and the professor who puts ideas into social action becomes as important as the professor whose actions result in academic ideas. When all are protected by academic freedom, the university becomes a more complete and potent moral force in society.

It is easy to protect the academic rights of the scientist who stays in the laboratory and the teacher who provokes no controversy in the classroom, but institutions cringe when it comes to protecting the rights of faculty who say, perhaps calmly, that they are going to take their scholarship into the streets. Ghosts of student activism rise from the grave. Faculty who would change society seem to differ from those who would maintain or even criticize it. Every professor should understand the difference. Even though a broad line separates most colleges from their communities and science from social reform, professors will not understand the full meaning of academic freedom until they examine what truth means on the other side of the line.

Faculty Service Functions

The service functions must be pursued as selflessly as research and teaching, but the rights of professors to perform these functions have not been explored. The functions include duties inside the university and outside—in professional associations, nonprofit agencies, and profit-making agencies.

The rise of the research university has been accompanied by a dramatic increase in the number of associations representing different disciplines and occupational endeavors. They have boosted the professional status as well as the knowledge of their members. They have offered faculty a range of involvements, extending from the administration of the associations to scholarly presentations of research.

Involvements in nonprofit agencies include administrative activities, as well as others that are related to scholarship. Professors sit on the boards of service coalitions such as health-care and religious organizations. They provide in-service workshops and research information, often through resources they obtain from foundations or state governments. Involvements in profit-making enterprises rarely involve administration except through service on the boards of corporations. The president usually sits there instead of the professor, but the presence of any academician raises questions about the responsibilities, benefits, and priorities of such appointments. Can a president justify a trip to a board meeting in Hawaii through vague promises of grants to the institution?

More frequently, the service of professors includes educational, research, and evaluation activities that improve the personnel, policies, processes, and products of the company. Unless professors receive exorbitant fees, most of these academically related services raise few eyebrows. The sole exception occurs when professors help create products for industry. Ententes between higher education and business can end in wars about who owns any materials that are produced by these agencies working together (deWinter Hebron, 1993). The battles are waged at the institutional level, but individual faculty are engaged when the dispute is about the ownership of any patents produced through the collaboration.

Most remaining activities outside the university do not involve the faculty member *as* professor. They are citizen involvements in which the professor needs to be accurate, exercise appropriate restraint, respect the opinions of others, and make every effort to indicate that he or she does not represent the institution. By fulfilling these obligations, a professor should be free from institutional censorship or discipline, but the AAUP Guidelines permit institutions to file actions against faculty whose external utterances, when viewed within the full context of research and teaching, disqualify them from faculty positions.

In summary, any academic rights in faculty service functions are determined by the scholarly or administrative nature of the functions. This indicates, in turn, whether the professor represents the society at large through scholarship or a particular agency for other reasons, through personal skills or the power of her position in the academy. A major additional criterion is the selflessness of the service, meaning the dominance of unselfish motives involving economic or political advantage. The institution and society should protect all activities in which the professor seeks to apply scholarship for selfless ends. These activities can move research out of the laboratory and teaching beyond the classroom. They constitute the final stage in the progression of the discovery, dissemination, and application of knowledge.

Administrators and Academic Freedom

Faculty freedom is determined by the scholarly and selfless nature of faculty deeds. Faculty cannot claim special exemptions when they provide administrative services to external associations and agencies. The same restriction limits any claims to special academic freedom by administrators. Administrators spend more time maintaining the institutions than the ideas of the academy. Each involves the other, but they must be differentiated in this discussion because of the political and economic authority of the institution.

At various times in its history, the freedom of the American academy has been challenged by religious groups that disliked Darwinism, business interests that opposed the curriculum, police who disliked protesters, politicians who hunted communists, and trustees who distrusted faculty. Today, there are several new and continuing political and economic challenges to the value of freedom, including retrenchment, a crisis in state funding, an agenda for national reform and accountability, the politicization of expertise, and research funding patterns that emphasize government-university-industrial partnerships (Slaughter, 1988). As authorities external to higher education try to control it, faculty lose their independence and their abilities to direct their agendas. They need responsive servant leaders who, though not protected themselves, attempt to preserve the moral force of freedom within an economic and political entity. Administrators serve as the protectors of academic freedom, and their stewardship must be honored.

One would think that faculty would respect such colleagues, but in many American colleges and universities, professional administrators are viewed as a necessary evil; they rule only with the advice and consent of the faculty. The fact that administrators ultimately serve a board of elected or appointed governors (and through them, a broader public) has been misunderstood or ignored by most faculty. Faculty contend that they should run their institutions, even though they have been admonished since at least 1918 to maintain slender ties to administration. During that year, Thorstein Veblen wrote his book *The Higher Learning in America: A Memorandum on the Conduct of Universities by Business Men,* in which he advised faculty to find administrators who "stand in the relation of assistants serving the needs and catering to the idiosyncrasies of the body of scholars and scientists that make up the university" (Veblen, [1918] 1957, p. 630). The service was not to the faculty as individuals but to their cause. They needed a free hand, which Veblen called the first and abiding requisite of scholarly and scientific work. And administrators gave it to them.

The collegial ideal of an academy governed by faculty, their sacred hand ruling secular functions, has been absent from most institutions for many years. Managerial, political, and even anarchical governance have taken over (Birnbaum, 1991). Academies with sixty thousand, or even six thousand, students are too big to rule by consensus, tradition, and research-oriented scholars. Administrators, those who "serve to" the needs of the institution, are necessary. These people must defend the value of freedom there, and many have lost their jobs trying to do that. During the 1960s, deans and provosts were knocked off the tightrope between student and faculty freedoms. In the 1990s, deans and provosts are dismissed who cannot resolve conflicts between traditionalism and multiculturalism. These people serve at the pleasure of the president, who serves at the pleasure of a board that might not understand all the implications of the value of academic freedom. The administrators must understand this value, explain it, and preserve it, but they do not get special protections for this service. Administrators are protected by common law, just like all other citizens. Their service to their institutions is filled with extraordinary value when it protects the academic freedom of faculty, but it has no special legal protection, despite its worth.

Institutional Autonomy

An institution can be seen as a rational entity, a meaning-producing system, a political system, an instrument of domination, an information processing unit, and a psychic prison (Morgan, 1986). It exists, therefore it involves power. The attribute of temporal power exempts administrators from special freedoms, and it limits the legal freedoms of the institution. As with administrators, the roles of the institution do not make freedom less valuable in the moral sense, but they do make it less available in the legal sense.

At some basic level, the institution of higher education must be free to find and share the truth. This identity comes more from the summed weight of faculty freedom than from any separate heft. It is based on the professors' responsibilities to their disciplines and, through them, to the society. If the institution protects these individuals, then it deserves to be protected from undue pressures. It survives as a valuable entity. The Sienna *Declaration of Rights and Duties Inherent in Academic Freedom* (International Association of University Professors and Lecturers, 1982) makes several connections between institutional autonomy and academic freedom, including the following: the university is a community bound together by a common commitment to the advancement of knowledge and the pursuit of truth; therefore, it exists for purposes that require a high degree of freedom if they are to be adequately fulfilled; and consequently, it is vital for free societies to have such free institutions, committed to seek and know the truth and bound to no ideology, vested interest, party, or government.

University autonomy means the independence of the university from external constraints in the performance of its functions. Academic freedom means the independence of the faculty from external constraints in the performance of their functions. The faculty must be able to accomplish their functions without discrimination or the fear of reprisal from forces that might be inside the institution but external to their work. However, faculty must realize that their individual freedoms and those of their institutions depend on the willingness and ability of faculty to keep the social contract.

In Chapter Two, faculty activities are linked with professionalism. One of the aspects of a profession is self-regulation, primarily through a code of ethics more restrictive than mere law. The institution governs who studies what, but it is bound as well by professional standards for programs. The institution vouches that human subjects will not be injured by research, but this standard, too, is often set by an external agency. On the grand scale, society lets its institutions of higher education manage their activities with limited control, because they have regulated themselves through professional accreditation. External professional agencies protect the ultimate public interest.

Accreditation and professional standards cannot protect public institutions fully when budgets are determined by state, federal, and local authorities that distrust higher education. At budget time, institutions of higher education do their best to appear as conservative as possible. No matter how hard the academies try, however, many people will view them as trouble-makers, even when their programs and institutions are "fully accredited." The history of the academy as an agency of criticism and reform is well known, even if the campus is quiet today. Just as the sacred church has struggled with this role in many societies, the academy as secular church has provided sanctuary to many social misfits and outcast ideas. However, the danger to institutional survival seems greater if this history is denied than if it is openly acknowledged. Freedom and responsibility synergize each other, and the society that understands the potency in their relationship is better served by it. When all of society's heretics are quieted, the academy is no longer free.

Student Freedoms

In 1992, the United Nations Educational, Scientific, and Cultural Organization (UNESCO) held a world conference on academic freedom and university autonomy in Romania. Two students from the Netherlands were there, eager to share a new, international statement about the rights and responsibilities of students. They sat patiently in sessions for three days. They listened to lively discussions at the dinner table, and then they went home. The discussion never found its way to their topic.

In most cases, and even in this chapter, the discussion of student freedom has been saved for the end of the meeting even though, supposedly, freedom in the academy has been split equally into *lernfreiheit* (student freedoms) and *lehrfreiheit* (professor freedoms). Each is supposed to have equal rank, yet professors receive royalties for writing books about academic freedom and reimbursements for presenting their papers about this topic at international conferences. Students have to make noise on campus to direct anyone's attention to their freedoms. The power of student protests is well known, but it often leads to legal sanctions rather than enhanced understanding about the rights of students.

The freedoms of students have changed in the American academy. *In loco parentis* limited student freedoms in the colonial colleges. The character of the student was molded and formed by the church-related academy. The typical first-year student was fifteen, and he had to attend chapel every day. He lived on campus and was required to take a senior seminar in moral philosophy from the president. Like a fish on a barbless hook, the student was held for four years, then set free.

The rise of public institutions and graduate education changed the curriculum and the nature of the student body. More, older, and diverse students enrolled in more, advanced, and specialized subjects. Students became less important than science. It was during this era that the notion of student and faculty freedoms arose. The German universities of the nineteenth century conceived *lehrfreiheit* to be the absence of administrative control over what students studied and where students lived (Rudolph, 1962). In Europe, few students have ever been forced to fight for freedom in places of residence or from parietal rules. Only the United States, a former colony, retains the regulatory vestiges of the colonial institution.

By the time the baby boomers enrolled in American higher education, they were considered consumers more than the products of education. Many significant protests took place at large, research-oriented institutions with more commuter than residential students. Society had given them the legal rank of adulthood.

Still, underneath the changes, most of these students were children of privilege, whose calls for equality were protected by their elite status.

Today, many young students are more underprivileged than elite. Many seventeen- to twenty-two-year-old students are ethnically diverse and economically disadvantaged. A significant number represent protected classes, even though their claim to that status is based on their vulnerability. Issues of student freedom contend with issues of student protection, not through *in loco parentis*, but because many of these students have been treated as a throw-away generation.

At the time of this writing, a truce has been called in the battle between free speech and the protection of students on campus. For a brief while, the proponents of civility outnumbered the advocates of free speech. What could be said about people was regulated. Nobody wanted fighting words. However, state and federal courts struck down most of the regulations, and the academy was faced with the issue of defending the value of free speech or coming up with costly and perhaps illegal new rules.

In *Free Speech for Me But Not for Thee,* Nat Hentoff (1992) warns about the tendency to limit academic freedoms in order to advance civil rights. A climate of fear is the product of such attempts. Hentoff quotes a reporter from the student newspaper at San Francisco State, who said that "students are afraid to say anything about a controversial topic that they feel could be misconstrued" (p. 154). Hentoff recommends verbal confrontation instead of repression. His favorite case seems to come from Arizona State University, where four African American female students saw a racist poster, confronted the people who made it, and led an open forum against racism. "After confronting the perpetrators of the flyer and then creating much of the momentum for what followed at the university they no longer felt like victims. They now felt empowered" (p. 194).

Conclusion: Choices

On the side of a pack of Camel cigarettes, Tom Robbins (1980) discovered this: "The word that puts the free in freedom and takes the obligation out of love. The word that throws a window open after the final door is closed. The word upon which all adventure, all exhilaration, all meaning, all honor depend. The word that fires evolution's motor of mud. The word that the cocoon whispers to the caterpillar. . . . In the beginning was the word and the word was CHOICE" (p. 31).

The key attribute of freedom is choice. Choice differentiates people. By improving people's choices, education makes them less equal and more individual. Their actions proceed from personal reflection and not from external pressure. Freedom and individuation walk hand-in-hand.

Unfettered individual freedom also raises questions about responsibility and about justice for all, the subject of another chapter. Toni Morrison (1993) says, "The function of freedom is to free someone else." This function makes freedom an instrumental value, not an intrinsic one. One person's freedom requires the liberation of others who are not so free.

Some professors tilt the scale of service toward their own advantage. They place the weight of academic freedom on their side, pronouncing, "We must be free to teach and study whatever we wish." They make academic freedom seem like a right that is beyond challenge by other values (Smith, 1985). This perception of academic freedom has led to its protection through law, but only because it holds a concomitant ethical commitment—responsibility.

Academic freedom is not academic license. It must be related to the truth in ways that serve the public trust (Brubacher, 1976). The 1915 *Declaration of Principles* of the AAUP acknowledged that there were no rights without corresponding duties, and, therefore, the freedom of faculty entailed certain correlative obligations. Research had to be conducted fairly, and students had to hear all sides of an argument. Teaching had to present scientific truths in ways that considered the student's preconceptions, traditions, and character development, and the profession had to purge its ranks of the incompetent and the unworthy who would not fulfill these responsibilities.

The measurement of true service is difficult because it extends beyond quantities to qualities. It is ethical as much as legal. Ethical authority concerns the maximums that all *should* follow. Legal authority concerns only minimum standards of behavior that all *must* follow. In tenure, accreditation, and even promotion decisions, professors and institutions are judged more by the titles, publications, and resources attained than by the quality of service inherent in such things. These forms of evaluation certify the ends but not the means and motives of accomplishment, thus they do not and they cannot fully protect and support the common good.

Professors must do it themselves, and in most cases they will receive more support for their academic freedom if they do. Most of their activities are protected by basic laws that protect the free speech of all. Their claims for special exemptions in teaching and research are increased when professors show that their economic or political interests are not primarily self-serving, in other words, that they meet the ethical as well as legal criteria of their work.

However, relative professional disinterest in personal advancement is a single, passive portion of a full, active interest in societal advancement—what Boyer (1990) calls the university's mission to reshape as well as serve society. The former shows an allegiance to truth, and the latter pledges an additional commitment to selfless service. Both are necessary for freedom to have meaning, but the challenges to the freedom of professors will increase as this form of scholarship is applied more actively within and outside the university walls.

Some will not receive tenure because they challenge the orthodoxy of their peers. Some departments will lose resources because their members are controversial in the university, and some universities will be punished because they stir controversy in society. Organizations and societies that are not free cannot suffer individuals who have earned their freedom to serve.

Chapter Five

Equality: Ensuring a Fair Start for All

The American Declaration of Independence declares, "We hold these truths to be self-evident, that all men are created equal, that they are endowed by their Creator with certain unalienable Rights." But is it self-evident that all people are created equal? It is obvious that all are born and all die, but we are *not* born the same, and each person's time before death is certainly different from anybody else's. If we are not uniform, how equal should we be? Should our rights be equal if not our conditions, and should we fight for equal opportunities and a few equal outcomes as well? The questions about equality involve its locations and life span, when and where equality begins, and when and where it should end.

I will raise the following points in this discussion. First, the value of equality starts with the needs of the social order and ends with the individual. Second, many types of equalities are championed and debated in our society, including economic, political, cultural, scientific, intellectual, moral, and motivational equality. Third, our society accepts the idea of equal opportunity, but the idea of *equal outcomes* scares most Americans. Fourth, new knowledge has boosted equality for new students, curricula, and institutions in American higher education. Fifth, the community college exemplifies the challenges that equality faces in American higher education. Finally, cultural equality, faculty authority, financial access, and a down-sized curriculum are continuing concerns about equality today.

Equality and Other Values

Three values are embedded in Western democracy—liberty, equality, and fraternity. Thus, the social case for equality comes from its linkage with the values of freedom and community; it is not a case for equality all by itself (Frankel, 1977). Equality keeps doors open; it gives practical substance to the promises of freedom, and it protects the hope for a new kind of human collective.

The freedom for each person to be individual is a goal of society, and equal rights are needed to accomplish that goal. American tradition holds that people need equal rights to become properly unequal, not to become identical. Equality is acceptable only when it does not mean uniform outcomes. People who seek sameness dislike diversity, and people who dislike diversity do not believe in freedom.

The value of equality starts with the social order and ends with the individual. It involves the basic ability of a society to provide for its members. If everyone cannot have everything within the group, then some decisions need to be made about who gets what. Equal rights at the outset temper the excesses of individuals and governments. Free people should not be allowed to step on each other's toes at the start of a race.

Types of Equality

The Declaration of Independence continues: " . . . that they are endowed by their Creator with certain unalienable rights, that among these are Life, Liberty, and the pursuit of Happiness." All Americans claim these three rights. They might claim rights to equality in economic, political, cultural, intellectual, scientific, and moral matters as well. However, the degree to which they take advantage of these rights is based on their individual talents and motivation.

Economic, Political, and Cultural Equality

Our nation was settled by poor people, and it still symbolizes the opportunity to be rich. Most immigrants are drawn to the United

States by the promise of equal access to economic opportunities. Few of them are doing well at home. They want to better their lives by coming here.

Political equality is intertwined with the opportunity for economic gain. Emigration to America became necessary for many Europeans who did not have equal rights under their own political systems. They did not inherit rights nor did they have the means to purchase them. As a result, America's founders rejected hereditary political privileges, honors, and offices. Washington turned down the chance to be King George I, while Napoleon became emperor only fifteen years after the French Revolution, when the masses revolted for liberty, equality, and fraternity.

Just before World War II, American anthropologists Ruth Benedict, Frank Boas, and others concluded that all human cultures were essentially equal. Their findings were used to refute the myth of race superiority that was becoming popular in Germany. Today's call for cultural diversity is based on the premise of the equality of different group traditions. Racism might be expressed through economic and political power, but it violates the American idea of cultural tolerance first.

Intellectual and Scientific Equality

The academy is supposed to develop intellectual ability, but that is a difficult talent to assess. Picasso was a genius and so was Einstein, but different measures must be used to gauge their talents. Different instruction must be used to teach such geniuses, too. If everybody has different intellectual functioning, then all might be somehow equal in this diversity. Are some people smarter than others? Probably, but the measures and morality of judging intellect have never been doubted more.

Scientific equality is the starting point in the discovery and transmission of truth. It is the first principle of process before the judgments of product occur. The search for truth begins with the premise that all things are equal until proven unequal. All hypotheses are tentative, and all findings are in doubt. Experimental findings will always be double-checked and, even then, they are subject to change because of new findings, new methods, and new sciences themselves.

Tolerance is the companion of scientific equality, and tolerance remains a virtue until the truth has been proven. It is not an end in itself (Martin, 1982). Pasteur admonished his colleagues to announce something as true in the name of science only after all adverse hypotheses had been exhausted. What then? In social science, especially, American academics have seemed to accept the concept of pluralism to the exclusion of all else. The absence of absolute truths has expanded to the toleration of half-truths. Scientific judgment is not being suspended only until truth is revealed; on occasion, it is being eliminated.

Moral Equality

The relationship between talent and moral worth is another issue involving equality. The value of individuation, which I describe in the next chapter, accepts the individual as an end rather than as a means to other ends. Each person deserves a fair share of human dignity. Despite profound differences among individuals, the full development of each—however great or limited her or his natural capacities—is equal in moral weight. Everyone, bright or stupid, large or small, shrewd or innocent, has a right to this shared recognition.

Abraham Lincoln said that the authors of the Declaration of Independence did not intend to declare all men equal in all respects. They did not mean to say that all were equal in size, intellect, moral development, or social capacity (Barrett, 1865). Not everyone can negotiate a corporate takeover, win the Heisman Trophy, or graduate from college. Those who can do so get more rewards than those who cannot. In our society, they seem more meritorious than others because of their innate talent or their hard work.

Are lazy and energetic people moral equals? Perhaps, but they might not be at equal levels of individual development. One of the assumptions of democratic philosophy is that all people want to become distinctive. This is their natural drive—the drumbeat for their march to self-actualization. But the evidence for this drive rests only in that state of humanity that dreamers like to dwell in—the ideal and natural state of humankind where people are free of encumbrances like political machines and assembly-line jobs. In this natural state, people share all the power and goods. All are born with all the advantages of nature so that all can become distinct human beings.

Most of our major declarations about freedom, equality, and justice are derived from this romanticized natural ideal instead of any temporal reality. Through these declarations, we have come to expect all people to work hard to develop their unique aptitudes. John Gardner's (1961) renowned example of excellence assumes the benefits of hard work: "An excellent plumber is infinitely more admirable than an incompetent philosopher. The society which scorns excellence in plumbing because plumbing is a humble activity and tolerates shoddiness in philosophy because it is an exalted activity will have neither good plumbing nor good philosophy. Neither its pipes nor its theories will hold water" (p. 86). The meek might inherit the earth, but the lazy do not deserve to.

Equal Opportunity and Equal Outcomes

Most discussions of equality start and end with equal opportunity, because it is safer to write about than equal outcomes. "Equal outcomes" sounds too Marxist to an American audience. Equal opportunity has been defined as the right to be socially successful if one is able, to have the chance to compete for success in a particular area (Lerner, 1976). Success is not guaranteed, but everyone should have the same chance to try. Success proves that talent prevailed.

Equal Opportunity

Equal opportunity supports the concept of meritocracy, that is, the rule of talented people. Jefferson dreamed of a society that was ruled by such people, some of whom would be educated at his University of Virginia. Ability, motivation, and courage would triumph over inherited wealth and social station. Political and educational meritocracy would make things fairer and more caring for all of the members of society.

The triumph of such talent is feasible when everyone is equally poor, rich, or otherwise at the same point when the tests of success begin. Then a few controls are needed to ensure that the tests are fair and open to everyone, and that people are graded and rewarded on the basis of their performance. But if the original condition of equity is not met, then exceptional qualities or circumstances may be required to make the opportunity fair. I describe these more completely in Chapter Seven.

Equal Outcomes

Most Americans do not believe in a society that provides everyone with the same power, authority, control, respect, and material conditions. Only the most radical egalitarians want to divvy the goods of the land into equal shares, dreaming that equal wealth will make people more cooperative and more likely to pursue intellectual, aesthetic, and physical activities for their own sake (Junell, 1979).

Such equity is morally and politically expensive, however, because it assumes that almost every inequality is immoral. Individual differences are guilty before they have a chance to be proven innocent, and the state must violate individual liberties in order to ensure the even distribution of goods and privileges. It seems that the collective prevails.

However, radical egalitarianism expresses the same overt goal as equal opportunity, that is, the liberation of the individual—at least in the nonmaterial pleasures of life. Thus, even the notion of equal outcomes does not include all outcomes; it just condemns material distinctions among individuals.

Some material products should be shared, because they are means for greater and loftier individuation. A person is more disposed to contemplate the spirit on a full stomach than an empty one. The children in a poor family will study better if the electric lights can be turned on. Any benefits to parents become the means to success for their children. Thus, the referent for equality becomes important. Some outcomes, even relatively stabilized, are means of fairer opportunity for all.

Equality and Higher Education

The academy has never been an Eden of equality, but it has approximated that paradise more than other institutions. To use the example of Bologna again, most medieval universities equated faculty authority with God's, but professors at that university were the servants of students. They might have controlled the distribution of knowledge but not the distribution of their salaries. Even the mediocre medieval university was more egalitarian than the society surrounding it. So was the average university of the Renaissance and the Reformation. No single institution was fully egalitarian, but new knowledge was battering down the doors of privilege from inside the academy out. Knowledge was specialized then as now and was represented by theology, medicine, and law. Even in the halcyon days of the liberal arts, the useful arts were competing for equal status.

The spirit of egalitarianism was pervasive in the colonial American colleges. The first colleges provided the liberal arts, but the curriculum broadened almost as soon as the pioneers trudged into the wilderness. Partial, parallel, and practical programs were more popular than ecclesiastical studies. The University of Virginia opened in 1824 and so did the first technical college, Rensselaer Polytechnic Institute, in Troy, New York. Oberlin College admitted women to study in 1833 and the first black college, Avery College, opened in 1849. The early American colleges were open to fairly large numbers of poor and middle-class students. Douglas Sloan (1980) writes that these colleges were more often than not supported by the entire community, were responsive to community needs, and were essentially community colleges.

In 1862, the federal government passed the Morrill Act and transformed American higher education by supporting at least one college in each state "where the leading object shall be, without excluding other scientific and classical studies and including military tactics, to teach such branches of learning as are related to agriculture and the mechanic arts . . . in order to promote the liberal and practical education of the industrial classes in the several pursuits and professions in life" (Levine, 1981, pp. 557–558). The practical curriculum was now equal in rank to its older siblings, and the Act helped institutions such as Cornell to become places where, as Ezra Cornell promised, any person could find instruction in any study. The new curriculum brought in new students, and among them were the tired and poor as well as the best and brightest. In 1870, higher education enrolled 2 percent of all eighteen- to twenty-one-year-olds. In 1950, the figure was 19 percent, and 40 percent were enrolled in 1964. Nearly 60 percent of all eighteen- to twenty-one–year-olds are enrolled in higher education today. Howard Bowen (1977) estimates that 75 percent or more of the population should be able to do college work at reasonable standards if further progress is made in improving the socioeconomic background of disadvantaged persons and the curriculum is broadened.

In 1947, the President's Commission on Higher Education (President's Commission on Higher Education for Democracy, [1947] 1989) recommended a shift in the conception of higher education as a privilege. Two years of it were supposed to become the right of all Americans. Concerned about the diversity of students, the beginning of the Cold War, and the new skills required by new sciences, the commission argued that higher education for all was not a nicety but a necessity. The vehicle of this new higher education would be the community college, and whatever form the community college took, its purpose was educational service to the entire community. This required of it a variety of purposes and programs: to remove geographic, economic, racial, religious, and gender barriers to educational opportunity; to provide programs that develop multiple types of intelligence; and to serve as an active center of adult education.

The equal opportunity commitment was sealed. Access and a diverse curriculum would attract and build the *individual* talents of diverse students. Thirteen years after the report, community colleges began an unparalleled growth of institutions, students, and programs. During the 1960s, new colleges opened at the rate of one per week, and today, 40 percent of all American freshmen matriculate into community colleges.

The Community College

The community college is the barometer of equality in American higher education. The offspring of father high school and alma mater, the community college has struggled to develop its own sense of equality and, thus, its own identity. On the one hand, it urges that all enter, be educated, and come out as good and employable citizens who contribute to the general welfare. On the other hand, it says that all may enter, but only a few will get into the best programs, fewer will succeed in their studies, and even the best will have to move upward to move onward. The first instance represents the interests of egalitarian secondary education. The second represents meritocratic higher education; equality stops with the opportunity for enrollment. Both are equal opportunity colleges, since both are geographically and financially accessible to students, but different conceptions of equality lie beneath this initial similarity.

The egalitarian community college embraces a comprehensive curriculum that is supposed to motivate enrollment and retention. Diverse programs make the college more accessible to students, and accessibility, in turn, increases the diversity of students. Ideally, all are educated to improve their vocational and citizenship participation in society. It was a democratic philosophy as much as a crude jest that branded the egalitarian community college the "high school with ash trays" in the days before smoking was banned in public buildings.

The meritocratic community college embraces some of the opportunity ideals of its egalitarian mate. It lets anyone enter its doors, but it keeps the academically unfit from enrolling in elite programs, and it weeds them out of other programs with its traditional attitudes, instructional methods, programs, and grading procedures. The meritocratic community college tries to be, as one critic once complained, a pallid imitation of Yale, but it must be noted that it is not fully aristocratic. It is a dues-paying member of the opportunity club.

Critics of the community college have argued that it has maintained the status quo instead of changing it, and the egalitarian model seems to be the major manufacturer of this malice. In *Second Best,* Stephen Zwerling (1976) writes that the expansion of occupational education in community colleges was an ingenious way to provide access to schooling without disturbing the social structure. Instead of equalizing society, the community college pushed the riff-raff into second-best programs and thence into second-best occupations and second-best lives.

There are at least five interacting ways that the community college could be charged with maintaining the economic and social status quo (Vaughan, 1980). First, education in the United States is hierarchical, and community colleges are at the bottom of the ladder. The diploma does not mean much, even when the adjective "community" is deleted from the name of the college. Many people know that AAA College was once AAA Community College, and before that, AAA Junior College; to some of them, it still offers CCC-quality education. Second, blue-collar students attend community colleges because of their economic and geographic accessibility, not because of their excellence. The colleges have no incentive to improve. Third, the students are limited to lower-status jobs that require only a two-year degree or less. These are technical not professional jobs. Fourth, an increase in the number of community colleges has inflated higher education, thus reducing its value. Finally, community colleges "cool out" students, reducing their motivation to succeed. Most students who flunk out of a community college think they have failed society, not that the institution has failed them.

Few Americans expect everyone to succeed in higher education. Therefore, the meritocratic community college seems not only palatable but desirable to many. Burton Clark (1960) considered the "cooling out" function to be necessary to a democracy. It helps people adjust who will not reach the highest levels of social attainment. Cooling out is a compromise among the values of equity, competence, and individual choice. Academic failure brings comfort so long as the people failing blame themselves instead of society. Whether people are cooled out after they have had a fair opportunity to succeed is another matter.

Meritocracy and Aristocracy

Sputnik was launched at about the same time that the community college was beginning its surge of growth. The Cold War in general and the space race in particular raised questions about the expansion of egalitarian higher education. The average American seemed to benefit more than the gifted one. Weak talent was overwhelming the strong at a time when America's best minds were needed to counter the Russian menace. As a result, the Cold War kept higher education from becoming as egalitarian as the high school; it was a matter of national interest.

Reputations and bankrolls were built through scientific research during the Cold War period. This cemented two of the three standards of academic excellence in American higher education—a good name and the money to back it up (Astin, 1985). The third standard of excellence—educational growth—was not as important an issue for the best research institutions. They did not have to work hard to develop talent because they restricted admission to the talented. Their students could grow on their own.

Continuing Concerns About Equality

Equality is involved in some of the most important issues of higher education today. Opportunities and outcomes are debated in cultural issues of admissions, the curriculum, and free speech. Faculty authority is changing, and tight budgets are squeezing student success and curricular innovations.

Cultural Equality

Cultural equality has affected admissions, the curriculum, and free speech. At issue is the extent to which inequality helps fulfill the values of the academy.

Admissions

Most institutions want to increase the diversity of their students, but someone is rejected for every person who is admitted. An African American is admitted to Harvard, and a white male with higher test scores is not. Asian American applications go up at Berkeley, but admissions do not go up proportionately; these applicants do not have enough of the "well-rounded" attributes of ideal freshmen. Equal rights and opportunities are at stake in both cases. Unequal outcomes are involved as well, because Harvard and Berkeley graduates mi̱ ̩t make more money than the rejected applicants, simply because they went to Harvard or Berkeley. Therefore, when the University of California trustees eliminate affirmative action for admissions, they also vote to maintain the socioeconomic elite of society.

General Education

The cultural equality debate has focused on general education. Some argue that the European canon has not included enough alternative viewpoints, while others contend that it contains all one needs to know. Stanford has changed its requirement in Western culture to a program that involves race, gender, class, and non-European cultures. St. John's has changed a couple of books.

Unless all courses are electives, some process must be established that determines what is to be included in the curriculum. However well that process works, it is subject to charges of inequity when any course or subject matter is required. The judgments made about subject matter resemble those about the enrollment of students. When Richard Wright is admitted to the circle of Great Books authors, another important writer is excluded.

Free Speech

Free speech vies with cultural equality in an emotionally painful debate. Caring people are distressed when students are pilloried for no good reason. Ku Klux Klan members, Farrakhanians, and drunken students do not seem to think before they speak—or even worse, they do. Caring people also tread carefully on the ice of political correctness. They do not want to be labeled as racist, sexist, or homophobic when they try to speak the truth or discuss alternative viewpoints.

Speech codes were supposed to take care of racist, sexist, and homophobic "fighting words" during the 1980s, but those codes were legally vague and morally questionable. They seemed to undercut academic freedom. In the United States, constitutionally protected but vulgar speech must be countered with strong, truthful statements. When "nattering nannies" protect speech, they put handcuffs and leg irons on the very freedoms and liberties that have empowered women and minorities (Page, 1993). Roy Innis denounced the "Schweitzer Syndrome" of whites acting on behalf of blacks: "You know why? Because it's important, first of all, for black people. We got to show black people that there are black men some place who can stand up to any white man on any set of terms and defeat him in battle" (Hentoff, 1992, p. 102).

Some good people will not speak freely about cultural groups because they are afraid of being labeled as bigots. Caution as well as value has become involved in any discussion about equality. Relative accomplishments can be seen as absolute goods or bads, and tyranny always fills any void of reason. The following illustrates the point. White men might outscore African Americans and white women on mathematics tests. Yet that fact does not make mathematics white or male any more than it makes it Asian because Asian Americans average higher scores in general than white men. Everyone, regardless of national origin, needs at least a minimum level of mathematics skill, which makes it reasonable to expect all educated people to attain that level of skill (Frankel, 1971). It is far more important to help everyone get this skill than to argue about which culture or sex owns the most of it.

Faculty Authority

The example of historical Bologna is an isolated one. The ideology of higher education asserts that students are not equal cognitively or politically with faculty. In the ancient and the contemporary guild, the faculty member is the master; the student is the apprentice. Not even student activism, the graying of the student body, and a consumer mentality have changed this rooted inequality. But they have shaken it a bit. When eighteen-year-olds became legal adults, they gained an element of equality before, during, and after the educational process. However, their litigious opportunities have not equalized their voice in the academy. To faculty, students remain the permanent underclass of academic organization—no offense intended.

No offense *is* intended. Faculty do not regard administrators as their equals either, especially those who have not had prior service as teaching and research professors. However, administrators, legislators, and the general public rarely accept the traditional notion that faculty are superior beings within the academy or outside it. As higher education has grown larger, it has also grown more hierarchical or even anarchical, and assuredly less collegial. The collective power of faculty has declined. Faculty senates do not govern the institution. Departments and unions have taken over. Faculty might be differentiated within departments by rank and tenure and teaching load, but most departments are equated throughout the hierarchy. During the 1970s, faculty joined unions in order to increase their political clout with administrators, trustees, and centralized state systems. This method succeeded for awhile, but unionization declined during the 1980s. The union label is no longer a tag of honor in industry, no guarantee of quality work, and no path to higher wages. Union membership has made faculty equal to stevedores and teamsters in the public eye. The cap and gown are simply another set of work clothes.

Financial Access

I have referred throughout this chapter to the impact of economics on other types of equality. Scarce resources have always affected the distribution of outcomes and opportunities. Even so, it is unrealistic to limit the discussion of equality in higher education to equal opportunity for students without considering how to extend fairer opportunities to them. That requires financial assistance for more students.

As more college youth represent the underprivileged of society instead of the privileged few, economic inequalities—and concomitant social and political ones—might become as important in admissions decisions as academic inequalities. Colleges both private and public have to increase their financial accessibility to poor students, otherwise they will not enroll in elite colleges and they will only enroll part-time in public commuter institutions. The first years of "Reaganomics" proved that poor students need financial assistance to enroll in elite institutions. Middle-class students entered public universities instead of private ones, and impoverished students entered community colleges instead of public universities. Harvard and other elite institutions suffered a major drop in applications of minority and first-generation students (Williams, Klein, and Foote, 1982).

Disadvantaged students need the benefits of residential, full-time study more than any other students. They need to interact with peers who are committed to college, and they need the time to develop all their skills. For this, they must have financial assistance. However, private college endowments can be tapped just so much to provide aid, and public universities seem to increase their tuition to the maximum legal amount each year.

Public education is becoming unaffordable for a significant portion of students without financial resources. What was once no-cost tuition became low-cost tuition. Now it is at levels that restrict admission and success. Students must take out loans to enroll in school. They must work more hours to stay enrolled. Both loans and working off-campus are negatively correlated with the academic success of students (Astin, 1977).

Down-Sized Programming

In addition, the curriculum falls back on tradition when budgets are cut. Curricular innovations are eliminated first, because non-traditional studies require marketing, materials, and management. It is cheaper to teach the liberal arts than any specialized, technological programs. Thus, a down-sized curriculum holds more classical thinking than creativity.

Programs for underprepared students are equally vulnerable. Remedial education is a necessity for most students once they are enrolled in college. It is disproportionately essential for poor students. Yet remedial courses are staffed by cheap labor, mostly part-time faculty, who are not available for academic advising. Academic counselors are assigned to mainstream advising. Their overcrowded schedules cannot accommodate extra time for these students.

When financial crises hit, inequities affect nonacademic programming and personnel as well. Student affairs budgets are already the most vulnerable budgets in the academy, so programs and support staff are eliminated. Collaborative programs with inner-city middle schools and high schools are canceled. Scholarships for under-represented populations are no longer available. Students with physical disabilities do not get rides to class. Even cultural activities are restricted to revenue-producing movies instead of experimental events that stretch minds and values.

Conclusion

The value of equality originates in the principles, priorities, and resources of society. Today, certain social groups are the focus of equality: African Americans, Asian Americans, females, physically challenged people, learning disabled people, and others. Individuals in these groups merit attention primarily because of the continuing relationship between their collective characteristics and economic inequities. Education is the means for improving their individual talents and, thus, their chances for dispersing throughout all of the economic ranks of society. The meritocracy is supposed to be made of individuals known for their virtue and talent rather than their color, sex, or political persuasion.

Today, "meritocracy" carries with it a sense of corrupt elitism, usually because of the entangling alliance between intellectual accomplishment, educational pedigree, and economic situation. Some advocates of meritocracy are no help, either. For example, in his defense of meritocracy, William Henry stated that "The dominant mood of contemporary American culture is the self-celebration of the peasantry. I recognize the towering snobbery of that remark, especially by today's egalitarian standards, and I do not apologize for it" (cited in Lehmann-Haupt, 1994, p. B2). The title of his book on this topic does not help either—*In Defense of Elitism.*

Opportunity must be defended more effectively. The defense is easy if first conditions are met. First, equal opportunity is efficient. The goals of a community are most likely to be achieved when individuals of talent do the tasks that promote those goals. Second, social positions should go to the people who can perform these tasks. Third, equality of opportunity is conducive to personal development. Finally, equal opportunity is conducive to personal satisfaction. People are happy when they can choose their life's work and perform the jobs they can do well (Galston, 1986).

Equal opportunity is supposed to let merit prevail over all other conditions. Like cream and hot air balloons, good students will rise to the top, regardless of their backgrounds. However, in order for this meritocratic ideal to be fulfilled, all social, economic, and political conditions must be level at the outset of the educational process. Too often, they are not. Academic and social opportunities are restricted to the children of privilege, handicapping even some with natural talent.

To serve equality better, the academy must help all students have full access to a good education. This ideal translates into access to all institutions, assistance with curricular and noncurricular opportunities, and the equivalent of a decent Ivy League education in every college in America, where opinions are treated tolerantly, expressed openly, and judged honestly as well. These should be minimal standards—even examples of mediocrity—in all academies, not the hallmarks of a few exceptions.

Chapter Six

Individuation: Human Dignity Growing

Which came first, the value or the institution? Individuation and the academy are chicken and egg, linked together by the history of the nation. The value has two features—human dignity and growth. Human dignity involves intrinsic respect for the individual, not respect that is measured by a person's usefulness. Growth is education. People grow into autonomous persons but not solitary ones. They constitute neither a nation of gunslingers nor of entrepreneurs but rather a nation of individuals who choose to live together. Free individuals create a greater commonweal.

Higher education does not make people equal. That goal is too low. Instead, the aim is to increase the development of individuality. It might be called self-realization, self-expression, self-control, self-direction, or self-actualization. It is not slavery, subjugation, or subservience. Selves are never slaves, stunted beings whose impulses have never been ordered into creative experiment (Brubacher, 1962). Of the self-evident truths of the nation, only liberty gives people the right to become individuals.

Individuation puts the "high" in higher education. It raises the academy above the proprietary school, kinder care, and boot camp. In *higher* education, people are educated *as people*. They are individuals, not just fillers of social roles or folks who do as they are told (Montefiore, 1988). Their wholeness is more than a collection of parts, but such singularity and completeness are difficult to achieve. e.e. cummings ([1955] 1965) wrote that to be nobody-but-yourself in a world that was doing its best to make you everybody

71

else meant to fight the hardest battle which any human being could fight, and never stop fighting. His words sum both the history and heart of the academy.

These are the major points of the chapter. First, individuation is a primary goal of the nation as well as the academy. Second, the education of character involves making an impression on the singularity, wholeness, unity, and responsibility of individuals. Third, the reform movement in higher education has reminded us that the education—and thus the individuation—of undergraduate students is the primary service mission of the academy. Fourth, the academy must involve students with faculty and campus life, and it must also give students time alone for personal reflection. Fifth, students today might be developing a second or third sense of self instead of that first sense that has been our traditional focus. Sixth, student affairs is an underutilized resource in the development of students as individuals; and, finally, the academy needs to encourage a gentle eccentricity among its individuals and institutions.

The Roots of Individuation

The roots of individuation are found in the political, scientific, and literary soil of the nation. These roots will be examined briefly because they support the value of the individual blooming above ground in the academy.

Politics

In 1774, Thomas Jefferson noted that America was settled by individuals rather than expatriates from England. These sentiments were echoed in the Declaration of Independence, and they resounded in the dominant political and economic philosophy of the day. Thomas Jefferson, Thomas Hobbes, John Locke, Thomas Paine, John Stuart Mill, and Adam Smith all believed that society was an artificial device existing for the sake of individuals and judged by criteria established by individuals.

These notions have sprouted radical causes. The social movements of America have been claims for individual human dignity as much as for the equality of women, African Americans, colonists, students, physically challenged people, gays, and other groups. In the 1960s, groups sang "We Shall Overcome," while individuals hoped *I* shall get to the top of the mountain; *I* shall see the promised land.

These notions have sprouted reactionary causes, too. Libertarians and Limbaughs (as in Rush Limbaugh, of radio talk show fame) want to restrict the role of government for the same reason that liberals have tried to enlarge it. Frances Moore Lappe (1989) has asked and answered the question, "What's the Surest Protection of Freedom?" "Government limited in both size and powers . . . [and] a citizenry of self-reliant individuals who do not ask government to take over what are appropriately their own responsibilities" (p. 65). These words echo Adam Smith's comments in *The Wealth of Nations*.

Democracy has been built by social movements that are based on human differences. Ultimately, these movements lead to the top of the same mountain, the principle of individual human dignity. Movements must fracture because they embrace difference. "Libertarian Party" is an oxymoron. Just as empiricism fractured the unity of reason, social movements must lead us eventually to the person.

Science

In Chapter Three, I discussed the fragmentation of reason into facts, followed by the rise of pragmatism, the American addition of action to truth. But William James and John Dewey were empiricists before they became pragmatists. They recognized facts as the outcomes of individuals in action. Dewey defined education as the reconstruction of experience that adds to its meaning and increases a person's ability to direct his or her subsequent experience. Dewey embraced the notion that the individual is never a means but always an end, worthy of respect for what the person is and will become. The individual is *the* ultimate fact. James said simply that education should be directed to what it means to be alive, to be free, and to create. Neither James nor Dewey thought that loneliness and isolation were the final products of individuation, but this was their faith as much as their science. By sharing their individual experiences and pooling knowledge, people would become more democratic, tolerant, and humane. Their faith in the moral power of the individual growing was never shaken.

By 1920, Edward L. Thorndike and John B. Watson, two of the first behaviorist psychologists, had turned such moral philosophy into quantitative psychology. To them and to their students, the individual became a collection of parts that could be examined using objective methods. Today, psychology offers empirical data about the personality instead of wisdom. To some behaviorists, human dignity is nothing more than the amount of credit a person receives from others—a sort of extrinsic, psychological reinforcement—instead of an intrinsic, ethical fact (see Skinner, 1972).

Literature

The American colonist's road led into the wilderness, the source and strength of peculiarly American myths. The first distinctive authors in this nation wrote about the transcendence of self through encountering nature. Henry David Thoreau wrote about self-discovery during a year at Walden, where Nature suffused him with love. A night in a jail cell reminded him that the individual was an independent entity from whom the state obtains its power. Ralph Waldo Emerson's basic principle was "trust thyself." His essay on self-reliance (Emerson, [1841] 1941) is required reading for any adolescent who wants an adult identity but is not hastening to find it. Life must be lived fully awake. People must explore reality through their inner selves. Do not listen too much to others, because society everywhere is in conspiracy against its members. Retreat for awhile, then return to the world. And do not worry about contradicting yourself, because genuine actions are good enough. Ultimately, the individual leads to unity. Unity was his hope, but Emerson admitted that he never found it inside himself or out there in others.

The Education of Character

The Greek word for character means "impression," and education for character involves making an impression on the singularity, wholeness, unity, and responsibility of individuals. People are not born individuals; they become them.

The Individual Is Singular

A person cannot be duplicated. "Character" means a distinctive, differentiated presence in the world, and talent belongs to the individual, not to a person's community or kin. Individuation sustains democracy instead of the barbarian order. In turn, it is sustained by democracy and by freedom, even though freedom means the loss of universal, objective, and imposed standards.

The Individual Is Whole

No theme runs through the literature about the goals of higher education more consistently than the education of the whole person (Bowen, 1977). Character activates a person's entire being. The individual is physical, mental, and moral. The sum of the parts means more than specific talent and intellect.

The Individual Is a Unity

One of the fundamental rules of personality development is differentiation. Its partner is integration. Nothing is truly learned until it has been integrated with the purposes of the individual and guided by character. Regardless of the many different types of modern psychology, the most important problem remains the unity of the personality.

The Individual Is Responsible

A person is responsible for self-behavior and, through the self, to others. Life is born when commitment, responsibility, and the knowledge of death are one. Each person is Sisyphus, and each must decide how the rock will affect his or her life. Outside forces are not responsible for how a person lives. Even though individuals are pushed and pulled by the culture in which they live, they will determine how far they will conform and to what extent they will break away from the group.

Taking responsibility for ourselves, in turn, makes us relate to others *as to ourselves,* as fellow beings in the process of becoming.

A relationship between individuals confirms the other as a person of unique value. Paul Tillich (1952) said that self-affirmation has two sides—participation and individualization. Participation means belonging to something and yet being separated from it and individual at the same time.

The Student as Individual

Individuation is the primary educational value of the academy. It encourages the development of whole, unique, and responsible students.

For the past decade, many writers have been trying to reform higher education. Whether writing from within or outside academic circles, they have shared the premise that educating undergraduate students is the most important focus of higher education. The in-house reformers have written in temperate words about increasing involvement and assessment and expectations in higher education (Study Group on the Conditions of Excellence in American Higher Education, 1984). The outsiders have castigated the academy and all in it for ignoring undergraduates (Sykes, 1988). Whether it heeds its inner words or those in the world around it, the academy must attend to this basic service mission—the education of students—and, thus, to their individuation.

The Student Is Whole

The student is a whole entity, more than a mind and just as surely more than a body. Professors should remember this, for they too brought their hangovers and hangups into the Saturday morning classes that they attended as undergraduates. Makers of movies about college life should remember this, for Greeks as well as geeks still go to classes. The academy is more than a mental maze or *Animal House.* It is more than a simple combination of those, too, just as an individual means more than mere parts. The parts interact. If sex is on a student's mind, then sex is an idea as well as a hormonal humming, amenable to critical thinking. If a student wonders about Aristotle's *Politics,* then a gander at Cable News Network any night shows how close tyranny is to democracy.

The Student Is Unique

Each student is unique. It seems ironic when the students who created rock and roll and relevant higher education try to impose their music and experiences on the undergraduates they now teach. The Society for the Advancement of Time has one simple purpose—to outlaw 1960s music in our lifetime. They are losing the battle. "We have met our parents and they is us," might be a modern parody of Pogo's plaint. Today's forty-five-year-olds fought the establishment in order to establish their uniqueness, but they seem to have forgotten their mission. They do not laugh at the existential joke that haunts them as parents—every generation tries to be different from the one preceding it, just as all children strive to differ from their parents. It is necessary to separate from the past in order to join the human race. But in the meantime, it is important to honor separation and the struggle to be somebody. No life is fully represented by a slogan on a tee-shirt. A rubber-stamped picture cannot substitute for soul. Each student is a work of art, irreplaceable and irreproducible. The stories that begin, "When I was your age," have had many more tellers than listeners. And these days, the diversity of experiences and ethnicities of students should warn most storytellers that they were never *these* students, regardless of their age.

The Student Is Responsible

Responsibility has two components—what people do and how people respond to what is done to them. Students build an ethic of personal honesty that grows outward into public life (Martin, 1969). Alexander Astin (1993b) notes that students who want to develop a meaningful philosophy of life are more likely to be involved in political issues and concerned with racial ones. In the process of self-realization, they develop common interests with other people because these are personally meaningful. Generosity emerges from giving as well as getting, and cooperation with others increases because it is based on a generous spirit. In short, college students become at least partially altruistic, giving selflessly from a sense of self.

Each student must learn responsibility, and because the student is an organic component of the institution, the academy is responsible if this lesson is not learned. Higher education is a reflection of students, it is an extension of students, and it is a resource for their self-realization (Fisher and Noble, 1960). The academy must involve students and leave them alone. It must provide them with models of social responsibility and eccentricity, too.

Influencing Individuation

Creative people have to spend some time alone. Genius is not part of the talent gang. But the prospect of being alone frightens most students, because their social tendencies are more developed than their selves. Yet, the time and place of American undergraduate education are reserved specifically for educational isolation. The traditional age of college students is set-aside time, identity time, to be used to gain self-knowledge. The time is spent better in college than in the school of hard knocks or on a therapist's couch. Ideally, it is spent in a small residential institution, where reflection becomes as natural as reflexive action.

Americans left civilization to find themselves in the wilderness, and many of their institutions of higher education grew up out there with them, in the frontier towns of Hanover, New Hampshire, Athens, Ohio, or Ithaca, New York. In those places, a boy could read the right things, think the right thoughts, find the right stuff, and become the right man. While only Doonesbury and a nontraditional institution bear the name Walden U., an institution by a pond is ideally part of everybody's growing up.

Today, most students in higher education are older, female, commuters, and part-time, so their time and situation of higher education differ from the classical circumstance. These students do not follow the guidelines of adolescent development because they are not developing a first sense of self that is centered on campus activities. Yet they have an equal claim on the value of individuation. Most adults are engaged in higher education because of an identity upheaval in their lives, usually a work transition that makes them look at themselves in a new way. Their circumstances collide like a comet with Jupiter, slightly behind the curtain of darkness but forever changing the planet. Whatever the reason for their enrollment and whatever their personal situation, the onus of the academy remains the same for these students as for their predecessors—to help them become persons.

The Need for Involvement

In 1984, the Study Group on the Conditions of Excellence in American Higher Education wrote *Involvement in Learning*, sharing with America what some educators had known for a long time, that individuals are more likely to grow when they spend time on college campuses. Reflection requires time alone and even more time writing and talking about ideas, problems, and dreams. Quality time should be splurged on the search for self. This time can be spent with faculty, studying the right curriculum at the right institutions, or perhaps with a cohort of student affairs administrators.

Involving Faculty

Many studies of student development indicate that contact with a faculty member is the most important factor in a student's growth and retention. The teacher is mentor and model. Both roles are necessary in the process of individuation. Students should have access to individuals who teach them about life.

At one time, it was the job of all American faculty to serve as models of moral development for their students. Since the president was first among the faculty, he was also the preeminent model. His company included Eliphalet Nott (Union), Henry Tappan (Michigan), Francis Wayland (Brown), and Mark Hopkins (Williams). Cleric, teacher, college president, and moral exemplar were one and the same person (Smith, 1956).

Times have changed and with them this role of the president. "University presidents used to address important issues. Today, they're mum on ills of the world." These words headlined a newspaper story about some invisible men and women who are college presidents today (Honan, 1994, p. B20). The example of Gerhard Casper is detailed in the story. This suave German-born legal scholar was hired in order to restore integrity to Stanford, but he has kept himself out of any headlines while performing his tasks. Casper has declared that a high university official cannot take a stand on an important issue without limiting the freedom of dissent on his or her campus. Less noble reasons can tie the tongues of presidents, too. For example, the president of Brown University has acknowledged that he and his colleagues are so concerned with fund-raising that they fear offending any faction.

Faculty are still responsible for mentoring and modeling individuality for students. They must still exhort, admonish, and inspire students to recognize the real demands of individuality. They know that great teachers teach themselves, as well as a subject.

William James fits among these teachers very well. He believed in individualism, and he modeled it as well. One of his students noted that James had an "absolutely unfettered and untrammeled mind, ready to do sympathetic justice to the most unaccredited, audacious, or despised hypotheses, yet always keeping his own sense of proportion and the balance of evidence." Another student said simply, "To see him was never to forget what it means to be alive" (Boller, 1980, p. 268).

James did not want to be associated with the Boston Brahmans. He was angry when his students did not recognize the talent and good will of people who did not share their social advantage. Each individual knew some part of the real world that others failed to see. Each had some specialized, singular calling. No one had a final truth or an unassailable insight. James believed that people could live together in a more humane world if they shared their individual experiences and knowledge.

Great teachers and great presidents still teach the meaning, the significance, and the essential validity of what they are about. They teach the processes and the motives of the subject. They teach from themselves to the students, and not just in classroom life but throughout college life for individual life. Their students are still unable to resist the one thing that mattered most to Woodrow Wilson, that is, to make the subject theirs for its own sake (Bundy, 1960).

Involving Institutions

The involving institution has the right mix of people and books and activities. It is a place that respects human dignity and helps it grow. The prototype of this institution is the small residential bastion of liberal arts. Others might replicate it, but none can duplicate it. In their study of small, private, liberal arts colleges in Wisconsin and Ohio, Allen Withers (1993) and Cathleen Morris (1994) found that the value of human dignity, defined as respect for the individual, reigns supreme.

Small liberal arts colleges have the size, configuration of buildings and functions, personal atmosphere, and classical curriculum that help people turn into persons. I discuss size and a personal atmosphere in Chapter Eight, but it is important to point out here that the purpose of the liberal arts curriculum is individuation, not homogenization. Yet, lately, the canon has been criticized for being Euro-centric, white male, white milk. Whether the classics in the canon fulfill the purpose, the purpose remains to affirm an individuation that transcends race, gender, and nationality. Many disagreed with his conclusions, but the initial premise of Allan Bloom's 1987 book, *The Closing of the American Mind,* was that the academy had to help individuals, and through them the society, to pursue self-knowledge.

When Nobody Else Cares, There's Student Affairs

The typical campus today is large, and its programs and people diverse. It does not fit the prototype of involvement. Instead, it provides specialized services and personnel to deal with the academic and nonacademic components of a student's life. They are called student services, or student affairs, or student personnel functions. Whatever their name, they are not always respected. Some members of the academy view these services and their providers as generally harmless diversions to classroom teaching. As I stated in Chapter Two, they have a mainstream educational mission, at least as far as the value of individuation is concerned.

The forebears of student services were faculty like William James. In 1918, seven full professors, all members of Phi Beta Kappa, gathered to discuss the moral development of students after World War I. All were deans of men whose meeting became the first gathering of the National Association of Student Personnel Administrators. A year earlier, the National Association of Women Deans held its first meeting. The concerns of the deans of women did not differ much from those of their male counterparts.

They were clearly the same concerns that John Dewey and William James were raising about the dignity and growth of the individual.

In 1931, student affairs was defined as a systematic intervention to promote an individual's development of body, mind, and character (Clothier, 1931). Five years later, W. H. Cowley (1936) defined the "personnel point of view" as a philosophy of education that puts emphasis upon the individual. In 1937, the Student Personnel Point of View was crystallized by a committee of the American Council on Education. The committee produced a document that stated that the primary purpose of higher education was educating free, whole, responsible individuals. One of the members of that committee, Esther Lloyd Jones, was at Columbia with Dewey. The document reads like a pragmatic conception of the academy. In fact, a few years later, Lloyd-Jones (Lloyd-Jones and Smith, 1954) wrote that the pragmatist philosophy—more than any other—represented the principles in which student personnel workers protested they believe (p. 12).

Student services became a separate area of the academy at the same time that the United States was engaged in war with Germany. During such a time, the faults of German empiricism were easier to condemn than celebrate. However, empirical science was given credit for winning both world wars. Just four years after the second war was over, the academic vice president of the University of Minnesota noted that his university had added scientific knowledge to student affairs work, raising it above sentimentalized intuition with strong overtones of parentalism mixed with common sense and good intentions. He said that science had also led to the specialization of student service functions (Williamson, 1949). This trend has continued. Today, an array of diverse, specialized services appears in every institution, their heft sometimes obscuring that central point of view that holds to the value of the individual student.

Student affairs administrators have an important educational philosophy, but many seem to spend more time with business officers, campus police, and legal counsel than with the teaching faculty on campus. They see the best and the worst students, the leaders and miscreants, rather than everyman and everywoman on campus. Some have even come to measure their success by the size, number, and prominence of their services, yet student affairs administrators remain the first potential contacts for involvement on every campus. Just as the Statue of Liberty welcomes the tired and poor immigrants to our shores, student service personnel welcome the tired and poor matriculants to their campuses. Their philosophy of holistic individual education should sustain those students throughout their time on campus.

The Need for Eccentrics

In 1957, Philip Jacob ([1957] 1970)complained that American students seemed generally to think alike, believe alike, and emote alike, regardless of their backgrounds or the nature of the colleges at which they were studying. Though written during the time of *Leave It to Beaver, The Life of Riley,* and *Father Knows Best,* Jacob's words still ring more true than false. In the 1950s, most students were categorized as collegiate, in the 1960s as activists, and today as multiculturalists. But in most generations, most American students have been vocationalists, unabashedly self-centered and aspiring for material gratifications for themselves and their families.

Jung said that each person is an exception to the statistical rule, just because each person exists. Where then are the eccentrics, the misanthropes, the individuals who find harbor in higher education? Where are the atypical academies to house them? Without such individuals and institutions, the conventional and conformist tendencies of higher education must prevail.

Student Leaders

The label *student leader* evokes the image of an extroverted cheerleader who heads a student organization while hurrying down the road to Babbitthood. The term rarely applies to a student whose primary campus address is a library carrel. That student's name is mentioned only at graduation, when an exuberant round of applause is supposed to make up for four years of nonrecognition. If higher education is doing its job, "leader" should be an equal-opportunity label that can be worn proudly by anyone who is becoming him or her *self.* Both gladhanding student politicians and solitary intellectuals must be individuals first, or their success is sham.

Faculty Eccentrics

The same is true for faculty. The faculty member as eccentric is rarely applauded except in old movies. Mr. Chips retired and the Absent-Minded Professor cannot put together a tenure portfolio. New academics have entered the tenure track too soon in their lives to be able to know themselves. They teach about other people, not from themselves. They study others' ideas, seldom creating their own. Their intellect might be considerable, but their wisdom and orneriness seem unremarkable. Perhaps it must be that way. Tenure and promotion committees judge a professor's success by his or her acceptance into the establishment, not by his or her skill with intellectual dynamite. That the successful student becomes the successful professor might be a tribute to conformity more than creativity. The tenure track can be a well-traveled rut instead of a singular road into the yellow wood.

John Brubacher (1976) writes that the only hope for the academy is when all scholars are intelligent, creative, curious, ambitious, diligent, and persevering. These dynamic attributes make eccentricity possible, even in a very young academic. However, the he or she must overcome first what has been called the Rosenthal effect (after experimental psychologist Robert Rosenthal)—the sickness of living up to a label, perhaps even one as prestigious as "professor" (Brazelton, 1989).

The Eccentric Institution

While much has been made of the diversity of American colleges and universities, the trend has been for internal expansion rather than the development of new and specialized institutions. The comprehensive community college and the multiversity are primary examples of this expansion, which might not promote individuation as much as corporate sameness.

There are few eccentric institutions today. Most have expanded their purposes, adopted comprehensive curricula, and followed the behaviors of prestigious institutions. In addition, public institutions have lost the autonomy that generates uniqueness. The drive for public funds has yielded existential similarity. Conformity provides security, but market-driven curricula and bureaucratic protectionism can squelch the distinctiveness of institutions as well as individuals. Warren Bryan Martin (1968) has declared that we have only one ideal for colleges and universities—the versity. Its variations are the miniversity, the university, and the multiversity. He praises the colleges of character, those small religiously affiliated liberal arts institutions that offer possibilities beyond those of large universities or community colleges. However, the colleges of character are disappearing, leaving the question, How will distinctive individuals emerge from institutions that lack a distinctive mission? America needs comprehensive higher education services, but there is slim guarantee that the nation is served better when every institution tries to provide every service. Instead, the quality of every service is likely to decline.

Conclusion

The academy sustains and subverts the larger society through its value of individuation. Even the most collegial academy emphasizes individual work, and the most isolated one prepares students for participation in the world. Individuation is important in itself, and it encourages the achievement of such other goals as preserving a common culture and institutions.

In 1962, John Millett said, "The goal of the academic community is to provide an environment of learning, not a product of learning. Knowledge is acquired by individuals. It is not an object to be built and used like an automobile, a piece of furniture, a house, or a pencil" (p. 62). Knowledge is a socially useful product, but no matter how much social utility knowledge has, the academy should still give the person something that is his or her own.

To create that special somebody, American higher education must embrace those people whose sheer individuality rubs off on others. Students, faculty, and institutions should be more eccentric in order to be more creative. William James said that our undisciplinables are our proudest products, but full-fledged individuals are seldom undisciplined or irresponsible. Self-discipline is necessary for genuine selfhood. Precisely because they realize their whole, inherent, unique bits of humanity, these individuals are more capable of connecting with others.

Chapter Seven

Justice: Balancing Freedom with Duty

The scales of justice appear in every newspaper horoscope and at the start of every police program on television. The zodiac sign of Libra is supposed to be the most balanced in the skies, even if that does not make any horoscope prediction more accurate. However, most viewers know that truth and goodness will be avenged on those television programs. The statue of Justice is shown at the start of them; she holds the scales in one hand and a sword in the other.

The scales of justice balance freedom on one side and equality on the other. On the side of freedom, people keep what they earn, and justice protects individuals from others. A just decision is measured by the dignity of the person. It favors what Kristen Amundson (1991) considers the *pluribus* values of diversity, privacy, freedom, human rights, due process, and property. On the equality side is collective duty, where individual freedoms depend on the social meanings of things. Here, justice is an obligation instead of a right, and it is supported by the *unum* values of equality, truth, authority, participation, and patriotism (Amundson, 1991). The needle in the center moves from side to side, weighing the liberty of people to do their own thing against their obligations to social equality. It wiggles between individual urges to be different and the egalitarian compulsion to be uniform (Conant, 1964).

Most Americans want the needle to rest on the side of the individual. Rights are more fun than obligations, because they liberate while obligations oppress (J. Wilson, 1988; Amundson, 1991). Two hundred years ago, Adam Smith pointed out the difference between justice and other social virtues such as friendship, charity, and generosity. People like to demonstrate the social virtues, but they feel tied, bound, and obliged to justice.

The needle might always rest on the side of the individual if not for the problems inherent in the last of the three great natural rights of life, liberty, and the pursuit of property. People and societies have different amounts of property, and that inequality raises the need for social order and justice. Since knowledge can be a form of property, obligations of justice affect all who own it on behalf of all who lack it.

The major points of this chapter include, first, that the academy has emphasized individual rights more than collective duties in its conception of justice. Second, justice is an appealing value to academics, because it applies reason to the problems of social inequity and individuation. Third, the acquisition of higher education can involve earned and unearned privilege, making it answerable to questions of justice. Fourth, the academy has made a compact with society that it will be fairer than other institutions. As a result, it gets to be self-governing for the most part. Fifth, procedural justice involves the rules of fairness. It fits the mechanistic realities of higher education today. Sixth, justice is harder to defend when it involves the redistribution of goods and opportunities in society, because this involves time, money, energy, and accurate assessment. Finally, the academy must take risks in order to increase the sense of substantive justice in American society.

Justice for the Individual and the Collective

The academy has emphasized individual rights more than collective obligations (Kerr, 1994). Individual institutions govern their activities, individual departments govern their disciplines, individual disciplines govern their curricula, and individual faculty govern their research. Faculty are nomads, wandering wherever they please in the search for truth. They engage in research, a somewhat solitary endeavor, and the institution rewards their research more than the social activities of teaching and service. Few are stirred to look beyond themselves when they consider the implications of justice inside the academy.

Yet many within the academy have fought for equality outside it. They have argued that any social inequalities need to be justified on good grounds, and most fail the test. The great struggles for social justice have involved equality, whether their specific target was the inequality inherent in slavery, sweat shops, voting restrictions, or other tyrannies. Aristotle said that justice was equality quite apart from any other argument, and the common Greek word for equality is closer to meaning "fairness" than the word for justice, which translates as "righteousness" (Vlastos, 1962).

However, justice is defined as fair play or even-handedness by John Gardner (1994), and fairness is its essence in this chapter. To be completely fair, justice wears a blindfold. She listens without prejudice, and she uses her sword with care. The Martin Luther King Center in Atlanta sells a tee-shirt with this definition of justice on it, "Conformity to truth, fact, or reason. The principle of just dealing for right action." Justice is as exacting as truth because right action is part of its make-up. This last attribute makes justice an appealing virtue for academics. It is reason applied. The terrible swift sword of truth cuts through social inequality to free the individual.

Justice, Equality, and Education

The institution of education is linked with social equality. America was founded by Europe's outcasts, people who believed that education more than any other institution could resolve inequities fairly. If all received a good education, then any inequalities thereafter would be the result of ability and not rank. Education was the great, first equalizer of human conditions, so it had to be passed around to one and all. This led to the expansion of access. It led to public schools and, in higher education, to land grant institutions and community colleges. As the needs of the nation increased, the base of education had to increase, at least until some people argued that increased access was fulfilling Gresham's Law, that bad money drives out good. Equality was triumphing over quality. America was not Lake Wobegon, the mythical hometown that Garrison Keillor describes on National Public Radio. All the children are above average there, but not in any other American town. How much equity could the nation afford?

Sputnik and the Cold War revealed some of the limits of "just education" defined as "equal education." To give quantitatively equal opportunities to students with unequal abilities was unjust to superior students, especially when the nation was imperiled. Plato's "people of gold" deserved golden opportunities, based on their capabilities. How much could society afford to waste the talent of the best and brightest by attempting to equalize opportunity for all? To many, this seemed just as unfair and undemocratic as preventing lesser students from exerting their fullest powers (Brubacher, 1965).

Is equality the ally or enemy of democratic justice? Plato argued that a just education is one in which every citizen is educated so as to bring out unique abilities and to benefit the people. The essence of this educational justice, then, is to treat individuals differently, not equally. Justice and equality are seen as eventual incompatibilities in this conception of these values. However, the lack of efforts to equalize things is equally unjust. The development of an educational elite has not been divorced from economic privilege. The children of rich families are more likely to go to college than the children of poor families and to attend elite institutions instead of low-status, poorly subsidized, public ones (Zwerling, 1976). Privilege exists when some people are permitted to do something that others may not do, or when they do not have to do something that is required of others. Higher education can be an earned or unearned privilege, earned by scholarship or unearned by social station. That both forms of privilege go together is understood by anyone who has tried to pay his or her way through Harvard. Community colleges might provide a great deal of access, but some call them second-best institutions (Zwerling, 1976) because they do not open doors to the chambers of the social elite.

The Dimensions of Justice

Most descriptions of justice include three variations on the theme of fairness—procedural, distributive, and substantive justice (for example, Bellah and others, 1986). Procedural justice concerns the fairness of rules. Distributive justice involves the fair allotment of society's opportunities and rewards. Substantive justice deals with the fairness of the overall society.

Some people might want to add retribution, what St. Augustine called justice for the unjust, to this list. Retribution evokes images of revenge and incarceration, the potential outcomes of any Friday night in a college town bar, but it does not evoke the image of contemplative justice, of mulling behind the blindfold about what is needed to balance the scales. Retribution concerns the offenders of fair practice, while this discussion concerns the providers of fair practice.

These different types of justice reveal the difficulty of making justice happen. The primary question of the academy, other institutions, and individuals is to what extent and how should justice reflect the law or go beyond it. In other words, does justice entail only restraint from injury (what medical ethicists label nonmaleficence), or does it extend to beneficence, to charity toward all as well as malice toward none?

Charity might be a mere act of justice applied, but some psychologists distinguish between these two activities, caring and justice. Caring represents an active investment in somebody else's life; justice is logic applied impersonally. The distinction makes sense to society's underdogs—groups that have been neglected by the mainstream; justice belongs to the top dogs, who use their wiles to keep the bones for themselves.

This conceptualization is simplistic, but it affirms distinctions between legal and ethical justice. Simple justice is legal, and caring justice is ethical. The law deals with social minimums for behavior, while ethics looks beyond those minimums toward what is individually right. Edmund Burke said that justice was not what a lawyer told him he *may* do but what humanity, reason, and justice told him he *ought* to do. Mark Twain said that his only obligation at any time was to do what was right, and then he added that this would please his friends and astonish everyone else. Whatever else justice might be, it includes legal and moral principles of fairness in order to be realized as a full-fledged value.

Justice in the Academy

Society expects higher education to be fairer than any other institution that it supports (Trachtenberg, 1989). Society has made a social contract with the academy: the institution and its members can be self-governing so long as their activities are proven to be just.

If faculty have greater freedoms in their teaching and research, then they have greater obligations to be fair to all. If they are guaranteed a salary through tenure, then they must use society's funds for just purposes. This begins with access to the academy. Faculty determine who has access to their property, knowledge, and thus to its power. They can use any equation for admission. They can say that entry equals the sum of mental ability, social expectation, individual motivation, and ability to pay, but to be fair, they must tip the scale toward mental ability and motivation. The other criteria are based on antecedent and alternative forms of property and power. Even then, faculty must be judicious in the ways they measure ability and motivation, for these too could be assessed unfairly. And this is just the admission process. Faculty have not yet shared their own property with any of these applicants.

Clark Kerr (1994) has stated that knowledge is not only power, "It is both power and money as never before; and the professoriate above all other groups has knowledge" (p.9). As a result, Kerr cautions the professoriate to exercise knowledge ethics instead of self-interest. For example, they must undertake research for its intellectual challenge instead of the money that is available for it. Temptation abounds. Kerr declares that the ethics of knowledge were in better condition before they became so subject to the enticements of money from the outside and to the intrusion of politics inside.

The temptation for professors to be unjust is not new. In *The Wealth of Nations*, Adam Smith ([1776] 1986) pointed out the even-handedness of professors at Oxford, who made a common cause to be all very indulgent to one another. Every professor agreed that his colleague could neglect his duty, provided he was allowed to neglect his own. The outcome? Most professors had given up even the pretense of teaching for many years.

In an example in Chapter Two, I suggested that justice determines whether Professor Jones should retain the income from a patent that he developed using university resources. Justice determines whether his combined income from private enterprise, scholarly foundations, and the people of his state is excessive. The overall fairness of society, as well as this individual, is at stake. If Professor Jones cannot regulate his earnings and if his institution cannot oversee his practices, then society will impose its own procedures of justice on the institution as well as on Dr. Jones. Justice can be a scalpel or a broad sword; the size of the cut depends on whether the university or the society is the surgeon.

The institution is able to remain relatively autonomous and financially supported because it has convinced society that it will regulate conduct within it. When this has failed, the institution has agreed to let reasonable external laws regulate its conduct. Most college presidents are aware that unreasonable laws are being drafted every day.

Keeping the wolves of unreason from the door is never an easy task. Institutions are more difficult to govern, much less govern fairly, as they grow bigger, more specialized, and more diverse. They are responsible to states, boards of trustees, alumni, students, accrediting agencies, athletic councils, unions, and political action groups. It is impossible to seem fair to all within and outside. Higher education should not take this personally; all public institutions face increased difficulties in governing themselves. Examining its different obligations to be just might not keep the wolves from their doors, but it might keep the wolves from getting too far inside.

Procedural Justice

In the academy, the focus of justice has shifted from an organic consideration of students, faculty, and administrators to a legal one. Students are not controlled by moral *in loco parentis* justice but rather by legal procedures. Administrators and unionized faculty have accepted a legalistic, adversarial relationship. Many institutions use legal personnel and procedures to ameliorate differences, instead of internal security officers and conduct codes.

Procedural justice is due process and guaranteed in the Fifth and Fourteenth Amendments to the U.S. Constitution. Although it is the least problematic of the three forms of justice, it still seems to take the most time. Rules are created and amended every day, a phenomenon that can be observed in any college financial aid office. However, time spent on the rules is straightforward. There is no need to meander into deep ethical thickets.

Procedural justice has been involved in discussions about the rights of faculty and students since the beginning of this century.

For example, one of the members of the 1915 AAUP Committee on Academic Freedom was Richard Ely, whose tenure at the University of Wisconsin was threatened because he believed that workers should be able to strike. One of the regents at the university charged him with supporting strikes, hobnobbing with union organizers, and writing utopian, impractical, or pernicious books. Ely had to defend himself at his own trial, but the subsequent 1915 *Declaration* provided information about due process for all other professors. Procedural justice protects students, too. For example, students in public institutions are protected against arbitrary dismissal by the Fourteenth Amendment.

Mechanical Justice

Procedural justice is mechanical justice. It seems appropriate to the empirical, large university. Things are not related organically there, rather they are divided by the procedures and rules of science. As a result, codes are drawn for every action. Faculty handbooks describe the procedures for tenure and promotion. Student rights are described in the student handbook. Both handbooks are scrutinized by campus counsel, but they are usually ignored by faculty and students until some professor is denied tenure or some student is expelled by a hearing board. Then the first words uttered are, "You have violated my due process!"

Manager Justice

Procedural justice is manager justice. If leadership is doing the right thing, and management is doing things right, then procedural justice helps do things right. Lee Upcraft (1988) writes that fairness is one of the six values important to managing right. The others are honesty, integrity, predictability, courage, and confidentiality. To Upcraft, "Being fair means dealing with management issues in an open, nonprejudicial way. If the best interests of the student, the institution, and the employee are in conflict, the even handedness of the manager is important" (p. 72). This means not making up one's mind in advance, and understanding all points of view.

Upcraft's admonition about listening before acting is not limited to administrators. It applies to faculty-as-researchers and teachers-as-managers. Keeping an open mind to all phenomena is key to scientific research; equality comes before differentiation. When a teacher presents all the alternatives to her class with equal dedication and honesty, then she is managing her teaching fairly (Wiggins, 1991). Put another way, a conversation is more likely to get at the truth instead of a monologue (Stimpson, 1994).

Equal Opportunity Justice

Procedural justice is equal opportunity justice. Fair rules prevent unfair advantages. Where people end up academically is independent of where they begin socially or economically. Equal opportunity procedures include need-blind admissions, in which admissions decisions are not based on the applicants' ability to finance their educations; nondiscrimination clauses in the charters of student groups; and the random assignment of roommates, with no consideration given to race, religion, ethnic background, or geographic origin. Policies and procedures such as these usually receive widespread support in the higher education community (Clement, 1993).

Subjective Procedure

The apparent objectivity of procedural justice can cover many subjectivities. Admissions testing is a familiar example. The Scholastic Aptitude Test and the American College Test measure achievement more than aptitude, and so, they are biased toward individuals who have had the opportunity to achieve more during school. The tests are not measures of native ability; instead, they reflect success within a particular environment.

Another example is grading. James Bradford (1976) asks why there are F grades when an E will perform the same purpose. His answer is that the F is an authoritarian attempt to add relative categories of student accomplishment. Yet there are objective F's, and there are subjective F's. I remember an elderly Polish man who came up to me at a community college. He held his English paper, and his hand was shaking. "Look, look, professor!" he said. His finger pointed to the big red F on the page; no, it pointed to the words underneath that F, "You're doing so much better; keep at it." The man bubbled with pride because he had traveled from FFF to a single F in a matter of weeks. Few Harvard students might have come so far in such a short time. His pride was unquenchable, and his grade was fair in terms of his accomplishment, but it could never measure his growth.

Distributive Justice

Sometimes the laws of administration do not give everyone a fair starting point. People do not receive just consideration according to their need, worth, or performance.

Creating fair opportunities demands more work than writing equal opportunity rules. Debow Freed (1991), president of Ohio Northern University, has said, "Policies and practices of consistency, whether in grading, housing policies, hair styles or in choosing whom to dine with, are often easier to accept than dealing with differences. . . . It is easy to be consistent, to establish rules, and to abide by them. It is much harder to be fair and more difficult yet to act with grace and generosity. This is our charge and our opportunity" (p. 9).

Some of the differences between procedural and distributive justice have been illustrated by Robert Brown and LuAnn Krager (1985) in a discussion of the ethical obligations of faculty. Although the authors related these obligations to the principles of nonmaleficence and beneficence, they seem to fit procedural and distributive distinctions of justice as well. The procedural adviser offers basic attention to students, while the distributive one uses student competence and information to individualize program development. The procedural instructor teaches essential course content and distinguishes opinions and facts, but the distributive one acknowledges student individuality inside and outside the classroom and helps students to apply the course content. The procedural curriculum planner ensures that the curriculum provides basic skills and knowledge, while the distributive one makes the curriculum current and responsive. The procedural individual in all these roles is technically fair, and the distributive one is more actively interested in the welfare of students.

Redistributing Justice

Before a college redistributes its opportunities or rewards, it must consider three things: the cost in money, time, and energy to do so; how it determines what can be modified; and its standards of measuring performance (Frankel, 1971). This requires more than redefining procedures or even compromise, which is sometimes merely injustice halved; distributive justice requires a case-by-case examination of actions and outcomes.

Costs of Distributive Justice

Money and time are the two major costs in redistribution. Distributive justice costs money, as any search committee knows. Flyers have to be sent to diverse colleges, newsletters, and interest groups to ensure that enough different types of applications are received. Equal pay is another example. It is imperative that people receive equal pay for equal work, but it saves money when institutions lower women's salaries on the basis of their rank or their college of employment. The same principle applies to part-time faculty who teach the same courses as full-time faculty. It would cost too much for some institutions to pay these faculty benefits, even if they are teaching a full load. As institutions respond to economic stresses and increasingly conservative political pressures, they will grapple with where they define their positions on distributive justice. It is important, as institutions struggle with this issue, that they pay enough for equality to happen (Clement, 1993).

Time was money to Benjamin Franklin, but no one has it stockpiled anywhere. It takes time to provide fairer opportunity, in advising, for example. Brown and Krager (1985) write that fair graduate advising includes being available, spending comparable amounts of time, and giving proportionately needed if not equal attention to students. The first behaviors are procedural, the last, distributive. The fair and just adviser is aware that the least interesting student might be the one who needs the greatest amount of attention.

Knowing What Can Be Modified

It is easier to level a football field than to modify most genetic abilities, so it is necessary to consider what *can be* modified for fair opportunity to exist. William Shockley—the Nobel laureate who argued that some groups were genetically inferior to others—has been silent for twenty years. *The Bell Curve* and *The End of Racism* rest on the 50–percent-off shelves in the local bookstore. Every day, science breaks down connections between ability and birth characteristics. Nurture still affects nature, and educators have always hoped that nurture might prevail.

The premises of scientific equality adjudicate decisions about modifiable conditions. Any judgment that persons cannot profit equally from the same opportunity is unfair scientifically and morally until it is proven true. Justice looks for the truth in alleged inequalities before rendering judgment about them.

The Standards of Measure

The standards of measuring outcomes are also a problem. Cultural bias affects discussions about a core curriculum at least as much as reasoned opinion. Multiculturalists believe the curriculum should be more inclusive because it is just to make it so. Such a curriculum reflects more accurately the diversity of students. It is no coincidence that some of these advocates represent the groups that they want to include in that curriculum. People want to study themselves. Others, part of the "minority victim's revolution" (Rothenberg, 1991), argue that this redistribution of content will dilute the college experience, because students will have access to timely materials instead of timeless ones. It is difficult to measure the proportion of reason, genuine concern about student outcomes, and cultural grudge in either argument.

The argument cannot be avoided, however. Someone has to decide how to allocate scarce resources. Some curricular selections have to be mandatory or else every course must be an elective. Changing the curriculum takes time and money. Thus, arguments about the fairness of the core curriculum are economic as well as philosophical.

Another illustration comes from the desegregation of public institutions in 1954, an event that harmed many historically black public colleges. Integration has made some of them predominantly white institutions. The point is not to argue against integration but to assess the outcome fairly. To what extent is justice served better by having some public institutions restrict enrollment on the basis of race because they educate those students better than integrated institutions? The ninety-nine historically black colleges and universities constitute 3 percent of all American institutions of higher education, but they enroll 16 percent of all African Americans and award over 25 percent of the baccalaureate degrees that African Americans earn each year.

The current argument about affirmative action involves similar questions. Procedures that are momentarily unfair might result in more substantial long-term justice in American society. Or they might be simply unfair. The academy will be one place where the argument about affirmative action should get most heated. Individuation will be used to support and oppose affirmative action. So will equality. All values should be welcomed to the debate, so long as justice uses her sword of truth to mediate the outcome.

Substantive Justice

Substantive justice is making things right. It involves the permanent rectification of outcomes, not just the redistribution of opportunities. It evens things out, once and for all. Max Lerner (1976) writes, "Rectification is the chief task of the fair and the just or at least of those who are institutionally constrained to be so. It is the least one can do, and far less than most of humanity can hope for" (p. 25). Distributive justice attacks the unfair barriers that keep people down. It contributes to substantive justice by helping people gain access to the institutions that develop their talents.

The "least among us" tests the presence or absence of substantive justice, but policies to correct discriminations against the least protected individuals in society can be discriminatory themselves. Although morally justified under principles of distributive justice, substantive justice looks least fair to the procedurist (Hooker, 1991). Procedurists argue that it is too radical and too egalitarian to give people goods just because their ancestors were abused. Even worse, substantive justice smacks of civil disobedience, breaking laws and rules because some people contend that they are unjust.

Paul Ylvisaker (1990) has identified three ways that higher education should promote substantive justice. It must renew its commitment to the historical mission of freedom and social justice. It must ensure that the campus models the ideals and practices of a free and just society, and it must encourage its members to struggle for freedom and social justice in the surrounding society. Professors must do more than spout facts. They must make society more just through the application of their facts.

This is easier to say than do. Although selfless attempts to improve society were lauded in Chapter Three, the problems of taking justice into the streets cannot be dismissed. As Kerr (1994) points out, the paymaster walks with the preacher. Political stances threaten public funds, and changing internal rules and procedures is more acceptable and often more productive than speaking out for external, social change. The procedurist would be happy with nothing more. He would answer the question, How does society ensure equality of opportunity? by saying, "By ensuring that the same rules apply to all, and that the doors are open to anyone who makes the effort. Anything more than this is actually an attempt to secure equality of outcome—a type of social engineering." But a commitment to social justice can require more. The social egalitarian would respond to the same question in this way: "Three ingredients are essential to make equal opportunity real—a floor of economic security under all citizens, grounded in the right to earn a living; a ceiling on accumulation of income-producing property; and affirmative action for groups hurt by discrimination" (Lappe, 1989, pp. 114–115). Both are at least partially correct. Institutions need to determine their stance on procedural and distributive justice rather than walk the path that is most convenient. Social convenience and social justice are not identical (Balogh, 1963).

In the chapter on freedom, I raised as an issue the case of students and free speech. This example illustrates the difficulty in protecting rights of free speech, as well as the rudiments of civility. There is moral justification in speech codes but not enough legal justification, as the Supreme Court determined during the 1980s. Yale struggled with this issue in 1975, when the Committee on Freedom of Expression (1975) differentiated what members of the community *should* say from what they *could* say: "No member of the community with a decent respect for others should use, or encourage others to use, slurs and epithets intended to discredit another's race, ethnic group, religion, or sex. . . . The conclusions we draw, then, are these: even when some members of the university community fail to meet their social and ethical responsibilities, the paramount obligation of the university is to protect their right to free expression. If the university's overriding commitment to free expression is to be sustained, secondary social and ethical responsibilities must be left to the informal processes of suasion, example, and argument" (p. 9). That last sentence is crucial to the just academy. Faculty and students must speak out in order to fulfill the obligations of substantial justice in the academy and in the broader society.

Conclusion

The range of social possibilities equals the range of human possibilities in a just society. In order to make this equation more real, the academy cannot rest solely on legal principles that protect itself. It must raise substantive moral questions about equality in order to serve society. Such questions will help give people fairer opportunities to become individuals. The goal of substantive justice is to build a social order of mutually empowering individuals. A community of such individuals is the subject of the next chapter.

Chapter Eight

Community: Mutual Empowerment

Community is a mom and apple pie word. It pleases everybody, even those who complain about their moms. But unlike apple pie, community comes in a wide variety of flavors. Higher education has at least the community of scholars, the community college, the student community, and campus-community relations to contend with, but the possibilities of the term have merely been scratched. More than ninety definitions of community are used in the social sciences—to characterize a physical place, a political unit, a spirit of human connection, or some permutation of those characteristics.

This chapter will include the following points. First, the human characteristics of community are most important. Second, faculty and students are connected in the academic community by their mutual participation in the process of learning. Third, while every institution advertises its community attributes, small, private, liberal arts colleges are most likely to provide the community experience to their students. Fourth, large institutions provide more freedom than community. Fifth, faculty are most important in the development of community; liberal education and discipline are two other means for the development of this value. Sixth, professional communities might limit faculty efforts to create campus communities. Finally, all institutions must personalize size, emphasize teaching and learning, and synergize administrative processes in order to build community.

Defining Community

Community can mean warm fuzzies or cold data, either the quality or demographics of college life. Community is important both ways, but the spirit of connection has priority. Woodrow Wilson said that a college must be a community of scholars and pupils, not only a body of studies but a mode of association as well. Its courses are only its formal side—contacts and contagions, its realities. The contacts among the members of the community empower each (Bundy, 1960).

Community is defined as mutual empowerment here. It is the glue that bonds individuation to equality and justice. Individuation is the value of the developing self, and equality is the value of the other. Community is the value of empowerment by each of the others. It fulfills the altruistic spirit and enlightens egoism. Community makes fairness to all the members emotionally imperative as well as rationally proper.

This community is not necessarily a place free from conflict, however. It is a place with open disagreements, or what Parker Palmer (1987) calls communal conflict in which the whole group wins by debating important issues. Palmer believes that knowing and learning are communal acts. They require many eyes and ears, many observations and experiences. Knowing and learning require continual discussion, disagreement, and consensus over what has been experienced. This is what happens in good science. Tolerance and mutual respect grow in the midst of disagreement. An adversary is, as well, an associate who is treated with respect so that coolly, honestly, and collaboratively, the best solution can be found to any problem (Harris, 1970).

Dennis Roberts (1993) describes community as the connection and support that enable the individual to take risks in the process of personal development. He calls this "social synergy." Robert Solomon and Jon Solomon (1993) call it "shared enthusiasm." Individuals enlarge their freedoms in a community; the educational benefits to the individual surpass any apparent restrictions due to group membership.

Every learner deserves equal respect in the academic community just because of the shared purpose of learning. Students are not just consumers, products of education, or legal equals outside the classroom; faculty are not just transmitters or discoverers of knowledge. All are participants in the process of learning, albeit different in their roles and characteristics. These differentiations are respected in the true learning community, and they are not used as a means of excluding the one from the other.

A different sort of community would be more polished, but it would undermine the individuality of the members of the academy, many of whom move awkwardly through the world as it is. A community that accepts the misanthropy of these faculty provides a healthy antidote to the rest of the world, with its grey-suited, buttoned-down, dressed-for-success exemplars whom students are taught to admire. Some professors will be, like Mr. Peepers, socially awkward no matter what, and the community of mutual empowerment will never impede their evolution as such. "The glory of their eccentricity, however, emerges not in such social oddities but in the intensity and focus with which academics apply themselves to their chosen corner of the world. . . . To study with people with that sense of dedication is one of the most important lessons in life, not the subject but the very idea of dedication" (Solomon and Solomon, 1993, p. 57).

The learning community is then not just a crafted collective but an artistic one holding the same properties as the art of fishing, which is like the art of writing and like the art of life, according to Ted Leeson (1994). In *The Habit of Rivers,* he says that the craft of angling is the catching of fish, but the art of angling is a receptiveness to connections, the art of letting one thing lead to another until, if only locally and momentarily, you realize some small completeness. It is okay to catch trout in order to let them go.

The Evolution of the Community

When people imagine a community, they might think of a tribal village instead of a global one, a place festooned with tradition somewhere out in the country. The elders impart their wisdom to the children around the evening fire, and all the village shares the meaning and tasks of life. Every member of this village is important, despite any specialized roles that each might have. The people constitute a whole. They are participants in an organic presence that began before time and will end . . . in the swirling turbulence of technology, perhaps. Modern society is high-strung and fast-paced. The megalopolis has replaced the village. People are automatons, whirring and grinding their ways from their assigned homes to their assigned jobs to their assigned burial plots. Each has a specialty, and when one breaks down, it—no longer he or she—is replaced by an interchangeable part. The innovation of the moment is more important than the wisdom of the ages.

Sociologists and anthropologists (for example, Cooley, 1962; Redfield, 1965) have studied the evolution of human groupings from the nuclear family to an extended one, the village to the city, the family business to the corporation, and the community of scholars to the multiversity. From thesis to antithesis—how far humanity has come reflects how much it has missed.

The *community of scholars* represents a small, ancient, and idyllic community much like any other. Early Oxford might have had many of its characteristics, and so might the American colonial colleges. Youth today need not forgo its historic charms, however. This year's applicants will have a community experience in any small, private liberal arts college. Just look at the pictures in any of their viewbooks: faculty and students eat together; students talk and walk together; and there's enough ivy to drape every building.

History might in fact repeat itself. Students in these small colleges view their educations very differently from students in other institutions. They feel more respected, more like persons than numbers in a book, more satisfied with their education, more involved with faculty and staff, and more convinced that there is a spirit of community at their colleges than their counterparts at other institutions (Astin, 1993b).

However, glowing descriptions of community are found in the catalogues of mega-versities as well, because of the allure of this value. Few parents want to pay tuition to turn their children into automatons. Dennis Roberts (1993) writes that he has seldom seen a college or university mission statement that does not put forth the "creation of a community of scholars" as a major institutional goal. The words are used so frequently that they do not differentiate one institution from another, nor do they compel a college or university to provide programs directed at creating this community. Alexander Astin (1993a) discovered that public research universities give the lowest priority to developing community, and they have the lowest student orientation among their faculty. Let the buyer beware. The large university is much like any other modern corporation. Its work is specialized, and its roles are rigid. Communication is difficult, and responsibility is diffused. People are alienated from their work, themselves, and each other in today's university. Furthermore, they feel powerless to change this state of affairs (Sanford, 1980).

The corporation metaphor took hold during the early 1970s, even though it can be traced back to 1918, when Thorstein Veblen wrote *The Higher Learning in America: A Memorandum on the Conduct of Universities by Businessmen.* In that book, Veblen railed against the business people who sat on the boards and in the presidents' chairs of universities. They had created bureaucracies that reduced faculty to the status of employees, elevated efficiency over creativity, and promoted size over substance. The mansions of learning had become places of quietism, caution, compromise, collusion, and chicanery.

The elements of the corporate metaphor are familiar. The academy is a commercial enterprise. Students can then be equated with consumers who buy knowledge, or with raw materials to be refined by knowledge, then packaged and labeled. Trustees are the directors, administrators are managers, and the faculty are salaried staff. These parallels with business can be drawn so convincingly that many argue that business principles and only those principles need to be applied to the management of large institutions of higher education.

The counterpoint is that large public institutions fulfill certain values of the academy better than smaller ones. Clark Kerr (1963) wrote that there was less sense of purpose in the city of higher education than in the town, but there were more ways to excel. There was less sense of community than in the village but also less sense of confinement. Jonathan Franzen (1996) writes about the freedom of the city:

> It's possible to worry, too, that young people who come to Manhattan seeking what I seek—literal centrality, the privacy of crowds, the satisfaction of being a fly in the ointment—will eventually be repelled by the miasma of Disneyfication that is hanging over SoHo and Fifty-seventh Street and creeping into the East Village and

Times Square. For now, though, I work and sleep in a building that houses two dressmakers, a realtor, an antique dealer, a caterer, and a fish seller. When I lie on the floor and relax by listening to my breathing, I can hear the slower respirations of the city itself, a sound like the rumble of a surf of subway trains crowded with people who are teaching themselves how to be here. [pp. 91–92]

The values of anonymity and freedom can be found in the city but not the familiarity and shared meaning that are everywhere in a supportive community. Paul Tillich (1970) believed that the city, by its very nature, provides what otherwise can be gained only by traveling—namely, the strange.

The terms *community* and *small college* are easy to juxtapose, but *community* and *multiversity* are an uncomfortable pair. It is easier to append *corporation* to Ohio State, UCLA, or the name of any other large public university. But even though the word community is used more often than its spirit is realized in any large institution, mutual empowerment remains an essential value in all colleges and universities.

Community Dimensions in Higher Education

The community campus is focused on learning. Its relationships and processes are organic. Some of these attributes were apparent in the description of St. John's College in Chapter Three. St. John's prescribes the Great Books for all students so that they can read, write, and reckon better. Students learn timeless, general principles that they can apply to modern situations. The purpose of their curriculum and their education is crystal clear, and it is the same for everybody.

In contrast, the technocratic campus is diffuse in focus and mechanistic in its relationships. The University of Maryland offers different functions—whatever society needs, whether it is teaching, research, or other forms of service. Curricula vary, too. There is no conflict between general education and specialized, vocational learning at the university, because there is no organic relationship connecting them. Anything is offered that seems useful, and if a program arm is severed, the heart of the university will not suffer too much.

The Learning Community

The small college is an educational collective. Learning occurs directly and indirectly there, inside and outside the classroom. Learning is holistic in its content as well as its location, because liberal education concerns the heart and hands as well as the head. Liberal education has always been moral in nature, because it links intellect with character and knowledge with action. Richard Morrill (1981) believes it is "values pedagogy" that should be the focus of undergraduate education everywhere. Values pedagogy includes moral relationships among faculty and students. Faculty help students to face themselves, to become responsible for their own learning, and to take themselves seriously as independent thinkers and agents.

Discipline is an example of values pedagogy. The academy has been allowed to discipline students because its conduct codes are educational, not legal. Yet Gary Pavela (1984) believes that discipline has lost its educational function in most institutions. He argues that consistent institutional values must be applied in all discipline matters, in order to make discipline educational. His suggestion would be difficult to accept, much less implement, in large, public universities, but it would be embraced as an everyday mission in many small communities of learning, especially privately controlled institutions. Some large universities might be content if procedural rights were protected and if police patrolled the corridors, but a small college makes student discipline part of its substantive declarations about justice. It might link student conduct with an honor code that outlines the responsibilities of members to their community of learning.

Faculty make up the pivotal group in learning communities, even more so than in large institutions. Donald Walker (1981) says that the faculty in traditional communities of learning have a sacerdotal view of their institutions. They are the priests, and all others are the neophytes. Faculty do not have to stand too high in the pulpit, however. David Riesman, Joseph Gusfield, and Zelda Gamson (1971) describe two faculty members at Oakland University who were warm and accepting of students instead of aloof. These two were not currying favor from students, even though it looked that way to more distant colleagues. They made great demands on students, but they did so with the novel attitude of good cheer.

Faculty are the primary group in the learning community because the educational mission places them and not administrators at the center of college operations. The size and service of the large university elevate administrators over faculty. Faculty take part in the governance of their institutions, and positive relationships with "official" administrators are a sign that the community is thriving (Astin, 1993a).

However, this focus on faculty does not mean that they value community at their institutions. They may lack interest in campus community as a result of their personality type, training, and competing loyalties in other communities. Professors in many disciplines are not very gregarious. They might feel more at home with books, microscopes, and computer screens than with other people. Second, the dissertation process encourages solitary study and professional skepticism, both of which are necessary for gathering research data but that also inhibit community. Finally, faculty may not value community on their campuses, because a different community has replaced the campus in their hearts—the community of the academic discipline. Academic scholars have acquired training and language that isolate them from others who do not possess the same knowledge and language. The value of mutual empowerment might be the same in the communities of disciplines, but the membership is more exclusive.

This is all right within limitations, but McGeorge Bundy (1960) says that faculty need two kinds of company—that of colleagues very close in professional concern and that of others whose notions of meaning may be held against faculty's own. Only through the association of all types and levels of learners can truth and individuals come alive.

The Organic Community

Cardinal Newman, in *The Idea of a University* ([1853] 1959), writes that the university is an alma mater, knowing her children one by one. The community is an organism, as natural in its functions as a family. Relationships are personal because everyone matters. Roles are general instead of specialized, and development is more natural than change. Smallness connotes synergy. People, actions, and interests are not merely shared in the community, they are integrated into its unique identity.

This collective cannot be manufactured from the top down. Natural communities have a high degree of social capital that endures over time, but bureaucratically imposed communities do not create what Machiavelli called *virtu civile,* the ingrained trust and cooperation that make the political and economic and spiritual affairs of the collective go well (Lemann, 1996). Like official mentoring programs, official community programs do not represent the free choices of the members to associate with each other. The most successful programs represent indigenous, participatory initiatives in relatively cohesive local communities.

Personal Relationships

A community is a place where there are no more people than can know each other well (Redfield, 1965), so a "civil community" should be a redundancy; no one is supposed to harm another member of the family, even though this sometimes happens. The value of personal relationships might be divided into two basic categories—mentoring and mutuality. Perhaps these should be called parenting and partnering, or senior and sibling, to connect them to relationships in the family. The small college is filled with family ties, and more than a few closet relatives.

Arthur Tollefson (1975) says that there is a direct relationship between the size of a college and the degree of alienation and depersonalization experienced by its students. He adds that many small colleges have used this phenomenon as a marketing advantage. To illustrate, the viewbook of William Woods College promises prospective students that the professor will address them and their classmates by name, and more than likely they will know all of their classmates as well. Nobody feels part of an educational community that has a sign flashing "Over 45,000 served" above its arches.

Personal relationships mean intense involvements among faculty and staff as well. Faculty and staff are as visible to each other as students are to them in colleges that are communities. The campus is an intense and intrusive experience for all. Just as students cannot hide in the back row of classes, administrators cannot hide in anonymity. Everyone knows the stars and the slackers—the exciting teachers, the deadwood faculty, the disinterested residence directors, the great accountants, the heroes of the institution, and the ineffective administrators (Komives, 1986).

Generalized Functions

The purpose of a liberal education is to prepare people who can think their way through any specific problems. Such people should find many role models in community institutions, especially small ones. For example, the dean of student development at the University of Maine at Augusta is also the director of the honors program. The chief student affairs officer at New England College is also a sociology professor. Faculty and administrators work near each other. They share the same dining area—both tables—the same functions, and they are available for the mutual development of each other, through a spontaneous debate about taxes or a pickup game of baseball. However, a jack-of-all-trades is seldom an expert in any, and a utility infielder rarely makes the Hall of Fame. Responsibilities in one area take away time from others. Some administrators complain about their divided roles in small colleges. Wearing too many hats can be tiring.

Specialization is correlated with both expertise and bigness, and America thinks that bigness is betterness. Specialization rules the university roost. It governs academic programs, business programs, and student affairs programs in those institutions. Specialized programs disregard the interdependence and interconnectedness of human problems. They dissect needs into discrete units, and as a result, they minimize the importance of satisfactory integration. A consequence of specialization is overspecialization; nobody has a clear view of the entirety of the human condition because everybody is too busy studying his or her own area of interest. Powerlessness develops as expertise disperses, and goodness is determined only by quantitative demand. As one critic charged, the university might as well put a sign on its doorstep: "Keys Made, Insurance, Real Estate, Notary Public, Antiques, Knives Sharpened, Lending Library, Pizza: anything to get a customer" (Caffrey, 1970, p. 258).

Change

A *college* is an assembly of colleagues. Change is a community decision. It involves the people and the purposes of the institution. Personalized relationships can be the cause of many meetings about minor matters. This is called *participatory decision making,* a natural style of decision making for those who dislike the task components of leadership. When applied to institutional governance, values pedagogy is the application of goals to all activities. The technoversity is not hindered by such concerns. Created by society, it adapts to serve society. Parts change without affecting the whole, and the rapid pace of change becomes valuable in itself in large institutions of higher education.

The large institution changes according to its nature: adaptively, mechanistically, and quickly. The community changes as an organism: autonomously, naturally, and slowly. Administrators dominate change in the large university, because they must respond to the standards of the broader society. In the community model of higher education, change is controlled by faculty standards. And unlike the case in the university, change is a means to other ends in the community of learners, not an end in itself.

The organism benefits by the additive nature of change, which might be labeled more accurately as *development.* Existing programs are modified; new, parallel programs are seldom created. An organism adds tissue gradually. It rarely replaces its arm or leg or heart. One change in the general education program must be carefully considered because it affects the entirety. In the large university, course options are added and deleted without any regard for their impact on each other. Individual students will choose the courses that are good for them, not the community.

Robert Brown (1972) remarked that too often the result of establishing new programs is continued strife, double costs, and even the eventual fade-out of the new program, once it ceases to be a novelty. He believed that the head-on approach of renewal and innovation was more painful and less glamorous, but in actuality, it was no slower than the parallel system tactic. A snail's pace of change can erect lasting structures, not temporary facades of innovation.

The Question of Identity

If it seems small, it seems like a community. Although some professional associations define a "small college" as any institution with five thousand or fewer students, this is an administrative convenience rather than a universally acceptable definition of the small college. A freshman from rural Ohio might think that Oberlin is massive if she does not make friends there. Another might think that a college with ten thousand students is small if she is used to living in a large city.

Few small colleges exhibit all the attributes of the historical community identity. The hard times of higher education have created new practices in some of these institutions, and new institutions for some practices. Since World War II, new types of small colleges have been created, among them community colleges and entrepreneurial schools. An organic educational focus is difficult to implement at these colleges because of the diversity of their students, their programs, their personnel, and their missions. In other cases, new curricula have been hatched in ivied institutions during the evening hours, in the summer months, and on weekends. Business programs, community education, and technical schools have been added at some of these colleges, usually to sustain their parents in the liberal arts, but occasionally they outgrow their elders. Half of all four-year colleges now offer degrees in business, and the number of master's degree programs in this area grew from 424 in 1976 to 611 in 1985. Seldom have the staffs, students, and courses of these offspring been fully accepted and integrated in older colleges. They are Cinderellas in their stepmother's house.

Small institutions should think twice before they impersonate big ones. Warren Bryan Martin (1982) charges that they become communities of convenience instead of communities of conviction when they do. But big institutions should work immediately to establish the value of community on their campuses. Robert Solomon and Jon Solomon (1993) speak for many when they declare that the university does not need more structure or authority as much as it needs an expanded sense of community and more communities within the university. Only in small communities are human beings known as whole persons, do human beings behave as whole persons, and do human beings find human significance and value (Lloyd-Jones and Smith, 1954).

Restoring the Community Value

During the late 1960s, some activists wanted to restore the sense of community that appeared to be missing from large, public "great society" institutions of higher education (for example, Newman and Oliver, 1969). In more recent years, other writers have resurrected the value of community in order to counteract practices in large institutions (for example, Sanford, 1980). The Study Group on the Conditions of Excellence in American Higher Education (1984) recommended the establishment of more "learning communities" at large institutions. Such communities build a sense of identity and cohesiveness among students. They integrate formal and informal curricula, and they counteract the isolation and anomie of students. One example of such a community is the Sierra Project for freshmen at the University of California at Irvine. Freshmen report that the sense of community helps them to develop moral character, feel close to the college, feel supported by each other, and become involved with faculty and staff (Whitely, Bertin, Ferrant, and Yokota, 1985).

In 1990, the Carnegie Foundation for the Advancement of Teaching joined the call for community. Their "community" has several attributes that parallel the values discussed in this book. The foundation wrote that a community should be educationally *purposeful*, in other words, it should have a sense of values. It should be *open*; the value of freedom must not be compromised there. The community should be *just*, which means that it should honor the value of individuation. It should be *disciplined*, in other words, a place that upholds justice. This community should also be *caring*; it is a place where service to others is encouraged. Finally, the foundation said that a community should be *celebrative*; and while there is no parallel for that concept in this book, this idea of celebration enhances the rest of the values. Celebration honors the traditions of an assemblage whose meaning is evolving over time.

A year after the Carnegie Foundation model was published, George Kuh, John Schuh, Elizabeth Whitt, and Associates (1991) published *Involving Colleges,* the results of their study of colleges that increase the quality and quantity of time that students spend on campus. As I stated at length in Chapter Six, involving colleges develop individual students better than other colleges. They also provide a better sense of community than other colleges, regardless of their size. Involving colleges offer small, human-scale environments and multiple subcommunities to encourage student growth and satisfaction.

These two publications could not have appeared at a better time. According to the 1990 Carnegie Foundation data, 73 percent of the faculty at research universities ranked the "sense of community" at their institution as only fair or poor. Only 43 percent of the faculty at liberal arts colleges ranked the "sense of community" as fair or poor at their institutions. Seventy-one percent of all the presidents in the study believed that a stronger sense of community was the most important factor in improving campus life at their institutions.

Implementing the Value of Community

At least three things contribute to the community spirit at liberal arts institutions: small size, commitment to teaching, and administrative leadership. These suggest three general strategies for implementing the value of community at *all* colleges and universities. They should personalize size, emphasize education, and synergize administration.

Personalizing Size

It is commonplace to blame the lack of community on the size of institutions, because large size changes the substance and the savor of higher education. Increased size is correlated with increased bureaucracy, specialization, and depersonalization. However, few cry out "Let's go back!" because most institutions do not want to become smaller. They cannot afford to become halcyon liberal arts colleges, nor should many of them try. As John Folger wrote in 1963, the answer to the problems of size is not to do away with universities but to overcome the difficulties that size represents. That means enhancing the interpersonal elements of any institution.

Arthur Tollefson (1975) believes that a college community has three characteristics that can personalize size: learning to know each other, peer influence, and territoriality.

Learning to Know Each Other

This quality transcends casual friendship. It contains a spirit of mutual challenge and acceptance among all of the members of the community. It breeds love as well as understanding. If mutuality is accepted by faculty, students, and administrators, then the challenges of learning together will be easier.

Peer Influence

Tollefson's "peer influence" refers to student interactions, but it can apply to faculty and administrator interactions as well. Peer interactions are a selling point for students. They can be encouraged by putting fresher candy in vending machines, MTV near washing machines, and a coffee pot in the commuter lounge. Peer involvement attracts students to colleges, and it helps retain them in the learning community.

Territoriality

Territoriality might involve the decentralization of functions, individualized advising, living-learning units on campus, and small-group instruction. Such structures and activities bring services to students on their own turf. They down-size the campus but with an educational instead of a budgetary incentive.

This educational down-sizing ensures that every member of the community matters, and nobody feels marginal. People feel that they matter when others depend on them and are interested in them. They receive attention; they feel important; they see others as an extension of themselves, and their accomplishments are recognized (Schlossberg, 1989).

Emphasizing Education

Woodrow Wilson said that contact, companionship, and familiar intercourse make up the law of life for the mind. The contacts and companions must include more than undergraduates. They must include the teachers, the people to whom life has revealed more of its meaning: "So long as instruction and life do not merge in our colleges, so long as what the undergraduates do and what they are taught occupy two separate, air-tight compartments in their con- sciousness, so long will the college be ineffectual" (cited in Bundy, 1960, pp. 29–30).

Politicians have called for a new focus on undergraduate teach- ing, and their call cannot be ignored, because it reminds us of the mission of the community. Learning is the mission of the full col- lective; it is not just a compartmentalized function of a portion of the group. Billy Wireman (1967) called the relationship between teacher, student, and curriculum the center of gravity of higher education. Research is a mission, too, but it is usually manifested individually. A few graduate research assistants might get a com- munity learning experience in their third-story laboratories, but that is rarely the case for undergraduates.

That politicians are not completely off the mark was indicated in the reaction of Philip Sandberg to a speech on community that Alexander Astin made at the University of Illinois. Astin had de- clared that the student-centered orientation of faculty was the most important factor in developing community in higher education. Faculty who cared about teaching and who interacted with students should be hired and promoted if universities ever wanted to de- velop learning communities. Sandberg agreed that teaching built community more than research, because it was outwardly directed and measured not by the success of the instructor but by the suc- cess of students. However, Sandberg also noted that "the inclusion, in recent discussions of the term 'student centered education' [in a statement about universities] strikes me as more than a bit strange—rather like 'diner-centered restaurants' or 'passenger- centered airlines'" (1993, p. 37).

Patrick Terenzini and Ernest Pascarella (1994) have discovered that the quality in undergraduate education resides more in an in- stitution's total educational climate than in any stock of individual resources. The impact of the learning involves six factors: the na- ture and cohesiveness of students' curricular experiences; their course-taking patterns; the quality of teaching they receive and the extent to which faculty members involve students actively in the teaching-learning process; the frequency, purpose, and quality of students' nonclassroom interactions with faculty members; the nature of peer-group interactions and extracurricular activities; and the extent to which institutional structures promote cohesive environments that value the life of the mind and high degrees of student academic and social involvement. All of these factors can be related to the presence or absence of the community value on learning.

A learning community is a day and night conversation (Solomon and Solomon, 1993), not one that stops at five o'clock. The community campus eats, breathes, and sleeps education. Terenzini and Pascarella (1994) define instruction as the important teaching that faculty members do both inside and outside the classroom. Research has linked informal contact with faculty to perceptions of intellectual growth during college, increases in intellectual orientation, the liberalization of social and political values, growth in autonomy, increases in interpersonal skills, gains in general maturity, orientation toward a scholarly career, educational aspirations, persistence, and attainment. The impact is increased by the content of the contacts and not just their frequency. Faculty should try to teach students in their conversations outside the classroom instead of just talking about the local movies. In sum, Terenzini and Pascarella write that the real impact of any college "is likely to come not from pulling any grand, specific and expensive policy or programmatic lever, but rather from pulling a number of smaller, *interrelated* academic and social levers more often" (p. 32); in other words, through being a community where everyone's learning matters.

Synergizing Administration

A cynic might remark that administration in some college communities has been synergetic for many years if the term means adding duties more than integrating them. The one-person office has become the one-person multi-office in many small colleges. Some of these functions are naturally related, but others are strangely wedded. At Westminster College in Missouri, the director of counseling also oversees academic advising and a program for marginally prepared students and has an academic appointment in the Psychology Department. The chaplain teaches half-time in the Religion Department. The director of financial aid is also associate dean of admissions, and the director of student activities coaches soccer and tennis (Remley, 1986).

Multiple responsibilities are not synergetic by themselves. The addition of parts means less than the integrated sum. Diverse responsibilities can drain faculty or administrators if they are not blended in meaningful ways. Patricia Cross (1981) has described two patterns of human development—linear and blended—that might be transposed to the careers of administrators. The linear model describes a sequence of developmental tasks that are engaged, accomplished, and left behind. An illustration of linear development is often noted in university administration. Student contact diminishes as line responsibilities increase within a single department within a single division. The blended career reflects small college interests. In it, student contacts are maintained, and departments are combined because of their shared significance to the mission of the institution. People are promoted because they are known. They manage diverse departments and activities because they are familiar with the students, are aware of the purposes of the institution, and perhaps because they fulfill the prophecy of a liberal education: they can see the periphery better than specialists.

The president oversees this symbiosis and synergy, but not by dint of any formal authority. At least two writers (Bergquist, 1992; Birnbaum, 1991) have noted that the president is first among equals in a community environment. The president persuades through informal interactions and through an allegiance to the norms of the institution, its mission. A well-drawn mission statement reflects the history and integrates the values of the community institution. It makes the president's job easier, as John Gardner notes, because it is very hard to lead a noncommunity: "It's very hard to lead a group of people who have no consensus with respect to values. I don't mean unity, I mean some common ground that you reach for" (1994, p. 193).

The mission must seem natural to be persuasive in the community. Richard Pascale and Anthony Athos (1981) write that great companies make *meaning*. Superordinate goals are necessary for corporate success, and those goals must be related to what the institution does best, naturally. Harold Hodgkinson (1968) writes that these goals are related as well to what an institution chooses not to do, that is, what it is selectively negligent about. Thus, mission statements are not just statements, they are the expressions of the fundamental values of the enterprise. Shared values allow diverse community members to cohere.

Few colleges die. They survive as nondescript mechanisms without distinctive purpose; the price of survival has been the attrition of distinctive meaning from their campuses. Too many good liberal arts colleges have become poor business schools. However, a few large ones have kept the badge of community. Arthur Tollefson (1975) includes larger institutions such as the Massachusetts Institute of Technology and the California Institute of Technology among the communities of higher education because of their unwavering devotion to science.

The mission statement contains the superordinate goals of the institution. It should minimize competition and maximize community (Solomon and Solomon, 1993). Universities have managers, but they need more leadership and the mission provides the means for it. Divisional planning, policies, administrative responsibilities and procedures must be related to the mission statement, that is, to the highest purpose of the academy. If the chief business officer and the chief academic officer have conflicts, they can appeal to the college mission, which transcends their offices. Even this process affirms the basic mission of the institution—mutual empowerment.

Conclusion

The value of community provides support for faculty and students as mutual learners who share the process and benefits of learning. Community invigorates both groups. That is as potent an accomplishment as it is rare, and as positive as it is potent. It might also explain why so many writers declare that the university is, first of all, a community.

Chapter Nine

How the Values Promote Scholarship and Democracy

Seven different values have been described in Part One of this book, but their impact is not discrete. Each affects the others as well as the academy. The primary example is service. It is the verb and the measure for its compatriot nouns: truth serving, freedom serving, equality serving, and so on.

The six remaining values represent two domains of service. First, truth, freedom, equality, and justice are most involved with the service of scholarship. Second, individuation, community, freedom, equality, and justice serve the democratic interests of society. These domains represent general emphases but not boundaries of the service of any of the values.

It seems easy to relate the scholarship and democratic values to the functions of research and teaching. The scholarship values are obvious in research, but they do not suffice. Research cannot be fostered or applied in a totalitarian climate. It must be criticized when it disregards the humanity that it affects, that is, when it is not fair enough and when it does not individuate people or serve the community adequately. Teaching is easy to associate with the democratic values of the academy. However, teaching is empty without scholarly substance and process. The scholarly essences of truth, equality, and freedom are necessary for human beings to grow. Individuals and communities cannot prosper with sloppy knowledge.

Scholarship Values

Truth is the goal of the scholarship values, supported primarily by freedom, equality, and justice. Freedom enables an individual to find and express truth. Equality supports people and ideas so that both can be judged fairly, according to their real merit.

Other authors have described scholarship values that relate to truth, equality, freedom, and justice. In *Teaching Values in College*, Richard Morrill (1981) offers a set of academic values that include precision, rigor, clarity, consistency, and truth. He also cites Douglas Heath's list of intellectual values, including honesty, objectivity, openness to alternatives, flexibility, humility, and respect for dissenting views. Martin Trow (1976) includes honesty, tolerance, respect, truth, rigor, and fairness as the values of effective scholarship. The middle-sized moral values of T. V. Smith (1970) pertain, too—scrupulosity, sensitivity, and sportsmanship.

These lists of scholarship values differ in number but not in their basic nature, and while the nuances of difference are interesting to explore, the lists share one essential idea—that truth can be discovered and transmitted only in a free, open, and fair environment.

Democratic Values

The political philosophy of this nation is reflected in the democratic values. Free people should have an equal chance to succeed, and justice balances the rights and obligations of each in relationship to the others. The goals of the democratic values are the development of the full-fledged individual and of the congregation of such individuals, but the individual and community are not just goals, they are also means for improving each other.

Richard Morrill (1981) writes about the democratic values of the academy, including human rights and human dignity, truth, tolerance, equality, respect for self and others, integrity, freedom, justice, and compassion. Kristen Amundson (1991) offers a list of democratic values as well, containing diversity, privacy, freedom, due process, human rights, property, justice, equality, truth, authority, participation, and patriotism. Both lists affirm the democratic purposes of the academy and the values in this book.

Preferences

Whenever individuals are asked about their values preferences, they seldom describe how their values really operate. Surveys make people rank their values one-by-one. Interactions among the choices are not revealed.

Any research about value preferences has another problem as well. It asks people about what they believe, so it is affected by the popularity and power of those beliefs. Survey respondents are likely to put down a mission statement rather than their real values priorities on the answer sheet. As a result, the researcher obtains information about explicit values instead of the implicit ones that guide the pencils of the respondents.

Faculty Priorities

Undergraduate teaching faculty might rank the democratic values higher than the scholarship ones. For example, in Allen Withers's (1993) study of academic chairs in liberal arts college, individuation is followed by truth and justice in the rankings of faculty values. Community appears near the bottom of the list. However, this finding might not downgrade the importance of community in these institutions, it just means that these faculty did not put it at the top of their surveys. Perhaps community is too pervasive to be noticed in a liberal arts college. Perhaps it would rank seventh on a list of 150, as well as seventh among these essential ones. Perhaps truth ranks higher than community in the small college, because liberal arts faculty relate truth to the individual human experience.

Research faculty should rank truth and freedom at the top of their lists, but few might relate equality to such choices. They might mark justice higher, because judging the outcomes of their research seems more important than the equality needed at its outset. Research faculty should rate campus community low, since public research universities are the least likely institutions to have a sense of community on their campuses. Research might require twenty-four hours of concentration but not the around-the-clock conversation that community demands each day.

Administrators

Administrators ranked justice high in one study of their values (Morris, 1994). Sound judgment is a cardinal virtue of the administrative craft. The community of the academy means something too, but the facts and figures of the institution—its temporal characteristics—compel this priority more than the idea of mutual empowerment. In two studies, private college administrators ranked individuation high and freedom low, perhaps because they represented small, morally directive institutions (Withers, 1993; Morris, 1994). Spirituality has its own dictates, as described in Part Two of this book, so it might rank higher than freedom in the minds of administrators in church-related institutions.

Students

Most undergraduate students favor the democratic values of the academy. They are concerned about teaching and the development of human beings, beginning with themselves. However, their notion of individuation can emphasize narcissism and materialism, and their concept of community can sometimes violate any shred of individuality. Capitalistic values are also described in Part Two of this book.

Every traditional student group—fraternity, team, or honor club—has elements within it that elevate the collective over the development of each member. The same judgment could, of course, be made for faculty and administrative groups, but the young student is emancipating himself or herself from group identity for the first time and needs extra support in the process. The justice of the collective might not be enough to emancipate the nascent individual.

Conclusion

In Part Two, I describe several values that challenge the scholarship and democratic thrusts of the academy. The values of capitalism, spirituality, and aesthetics dare the academy to be true to its own values and, as well, to modify those values in the face of other imperatives.

Challenges to Our Values

Part Two describes the challenges that capitalism, spirituality, and aesthetics pose to the values we prize, along with gravitation—the invisible force that draws the academy toward its challengers. The academy gravitates toward capitalism because it is an economic and political *institution* that must relate to its peers. However, the academy is also a generator of *ideas* that must relate to the ultimate values of beauty and good. Capitalism challenges the realities of the academy, while the ultimate values challenge its ideals.

Chapter Ten

Capitalism: The Challenges of the Material

The working title for this chapter was "Cinderella's Evil Stepsister," but I discarded that title early. It might have convinced a few cynics to read my next words, but it would have misdirected most readers through its oversimplification. An example illustrates this point. Steve Tozer was one of several people who responded to a 1993 speech that Alexander Astin gave on the topic of community (Astin, 1993a). Professor Tozer (1993) wanted to pillory Mr. Astin's remarks in an utterly charming way, thus turning his own remarks into material for a publication. He restrained himself. He said that this type of commentary might be confirmed by inattentive listeners or subsequent readers as the whole truth about community (or here, about the capitalist values of the academy), and not just a grain of it.

The academy is surrounded by capitalist values. Students come in with them, and they find them rewarded in their work lives when they leave. American universities reflect the capitalist values in our society, in part because all of them want to stay in business. Some capitalist values threaten the service of the academy, but others are "bourgeois virtues," positive manifestations that build institutions, faculty, students, and administrators.

Academies have functioned as businesses for more than three hundred years, beginning with the Dissenting Academies of England. These colleges operated on a fee-paying basis as commercial enterprises. They reinforced the notion that holy salvation could be achieved through business success; God appreciates hard work. Their faculty taught shorthand (for copying sermons), business accounts, and practical science (de Winter Hebron, 1993). In the nineteenth century, American academies flowered with vocational purpose. The Morrill Acts stimulated the development of trained personnel in agriculture and the mechanical arts. During the last one hundred years, American boards of trustees have been dominated by business donors rather than religious leaders. For example, Leslie Wexner, chair of the board of trustees of Ohio State, has donated $25 million to that institution. The members of the boards have advocated the use of business principles and practices as the standard of academic management. Capitalists have capitalistic values, as most presidents know very well.

All colleges and universities have been affected by the corporate realities of institutional life. However, none have to accept all the values of capitalism in order to conduct their work, and some of those values seem antithetical to the ones that have been presented thus far. They will not be listed in this chapter in one-on-one opposition to community, justice, freedom, truth, equality, individuation, and altruism, but the sisters materialism, narcissism, competitiveness, vocationalism, conformity, and consumerism might keep Cinderella from getting to the ball. After these values are described, kinder and gentler capitalist values are described: altruistic egoism, enterprise, and bourgeois community.

The Capitalist Values

Marilyn Ferguson (1980) has provided a list of modern economic assumptions that sound very much like capitalist values: consumption at all costs, conformity to the job, hierarchy, bureaucracy, fragmented work roles, identification with the job or profession, competition, separated work and play, the manipulation and dominance of nature, struggle for security, quantitative symbols of success, materialism, polarized labor and management roles, exploitation of limited resources, rational models of analysis, emphasis on short-term solutions, runaway uses of technology, and the treatment of symptoms rather than the whole. These values sound pretty bleak and bare by themselves, but their interaction with academic values can make them seem even worse.

In his address on community, Alexander Astin (1993a) commented that the values of materialism, competitiveness, and narcissism are emphasized more than community in many institutions. These are capitalist values that oppose such things as generosity, fairness, patriotism, social responsibility, and respect for the rights of others. The value of community softens capitalistic tendencies. The other values of the academy do, too. Individuation opposes conformity and the separation of tasks from life. Truth is more than material; truth-seekers follow the way and light of reason. Equality and justice wrestle tag-team against unreasonable competition.

Still, Cinderella as the academy needs to be careful treading around her stepsisters' beliefs. In this chapter, I try to guide her steps through the following points: first, that materialism offers many pleasures in a world of diverse and abstract truths. Second, narcissism is the partner of materialism. Third, competitive excellence is taught throughout society and the academy. Fourth, students of all ages are vocationalists. Fifth, conformity is encouraged at all levels of the academy. Sixth, consumerism has confirmed and conformed the vocational curriculum. Seventh, bourgeois virtues such as altruistic egoism are more natural for many than selfless service. Finally, enterprise and cooperation can be the product of competition. A bourgeois community is often created in the academy.

Materialism

Materialism is the focal point of capitalism but no more so than it is for Marxism or any other economic theory. Economics offers one kind of truth—a tangible quantity lacking ethereal beauty, the spirit of God, or the abstractness of reason. Material truths might set you free, but only if you use them to ransom your way out.

Materialists measure academic success by the amount and quality of tangible goods re_ived, whether it is the number of books they have read, the status of the stickers they put on the rear windows of their cars, or the salaries that alumni earn. What does the term *good college* mean? It means the material advantages earned through attendance at that college and graduation from it.

Materialism provides comfort in a world of multiple truths. No absolute unifying truth can be found out there in the world of academic ideas. Seekers who cannot be wise in such a world might as well make themselves comfortable. This is the capitalist corollary of empirical truth. Economic worth—which is capitalistic truth—

is measured by the number of things people own or their worth in quantities of dollars, instead of how much they know.

Since people cannot be well known by others in a large university, psychological identity there depends on all sorts of impersonal authentifications. Grade point averages, student awards, and even good tickets to the basketball game substitute for inner development. The curriculum suffers the same identity problem. Material measures replace internal confidence. A degree in business becomes better than a degree in humanities because it provides more income to the graduate and to the institution: more students enroll in business, more courses are offered, and more faculty are hired. Quantity counts.

Ferguson (1980) contends that the failure of economic philosophies is based on their emphasis on the external rather than the internal. This tendency leads liberal critics to argue that capitalists value an individual's wealth more than they value the person who carries the wallet. The person without wealth can sleep on the street. Material matters, not individuals. However, conservative voices counter that capitalism succors individuality by creating the material goods and freedom that people need. It helps them have jobs, develop themselves, and help others if they choose. Capitalism values their self-direction and initiative (Lappe, 1989).

Narcissism

The liberal is unappeased. Unbridled capitalism seems to foster narcissism more than individuation. Narcissism differs from individuation because neither the dignity of others nor their growing is considered. Our narcissist stepsister might include autonomy, tolerance, and personal freedom in her values lexicon, but the democratic values of service and community will not be found there. The narcissist uses her education to master subject matter, but she does not see any relationship between her subject and her subjective self, much less the selves of others.

Such a person is a commuter member of a profit-making collection and not a resident of a life-long learning community. Narcissism is self-imposed isolation. It cannot sustain a social order, because it and its attendant values of material success and competitive achievement derogate human connection and commitment (Montefiore, 1988). Narcissism fits materialism like a wet sock fits a foot. Together, they manufacture the fungus greed.

The narcissist is not an altruist nor even an ethical egoist, just an egoist—a talented one, perhaps, but the virtue of the good citizen is not within her. Jefferson declared that individual and collective virtue was what the talents must serve, but this stepsister will graduate without worrying about that. Her self-interest is as pure as the unselfish interest of the altruist. The narcissist agrees with Machiavelli that human relations are up for sale, because people are "ungrateful, voluble, dissemblers, anxious to avoid danger and covetous of gain; as long as you benefit them, they are entirely yours; they offer you their blood, their goods, their life, and their children" (Machiavelli, [1532] 1980, p. 90).

Recently, Peter Diamandopoulos, president of Adelphi College, has been accused of capitalist narcissism. A self-proclaimed businessman who claims to invest in things to enhance the elegance of his institution, Diamandopoulos is also the second-highest-paid president in the United States, with a salary of $523,636 in 1994. In addition, Adelphi reimbursed him $625,289 for expenses, including trips to Greece, and $15,675 for tips to employees at a million-dollar condominium that the university maintains for him. Student enrollment has dropped 25 percent over the past decade, faculty have voted for his ouster, and the New York State attorney general has subpoenaed President Diamandopoulos about his "extraordinary personal spending" (Judson, 1996).

Competitiveness

Every fall, students rush to the bookstore to see where their institutions and programs rank in *U.S. News and World Report*'s annual "Report on America's Best Colleges." Some have to push aside administrators and faculty to get to the magazines. A positive ranking means dollars to the institutions and top jobs to their graduates. This is capitalism at work.

The rankings measure what have been cited earlier as the reputation and resources models of academic excellence (Astin, 1985). Resources are up for grabs. They spark competition among universities and within universities in departments and within departments in subspecialties. Research competitions bring in new resources and enhance institutional, departmental, and faculty reputations. Faculty are tenured and promoted because of the dollars they produce. The fittest survive.

A capitalist democracy rewards the winners of competitions measured by objective standards. Adam Smith believed that only the invisible hand of competition should serve as an economic regulator. Our superiority as a culture is based on the triumph of some individuals over others, and the degree of their triumph is measured by the booty they bring home. This lesson is displayed every day in newspapers, television, and movies. Students come to college well-schooled in that lesson, and they leave better educated in it. High grades are more important than learning. Cut-throat behaviors get students through cut-throat classes. All this is necessary to survive in the "real world," where the value of competition is rewarded with money and power.

Vocationalism

A few years ago, "narcissism" seemed to be stamped on every student's identification card. In 1978, the Carnegie Council on Policy Studies surveyed student affairs administrators at 586 colleges and universities and found these phrases applied to students: career-oriented, concerned with self, concerned with material success, well groomed, and practical. Students were not just narcissistic, they were vocational narcissists (Levine, 1980).

There is some evidence that the vocational narcissism of the 1980s has abated, and students are becoming interested again in such things as a philosophy of life as well as a meaningful career. But it is no aberrant condition that students want material and professional success, nor that they attend college for a practical education instead of a general one, especially first-generation impoverished students. Material advantage is a basic motivator in the American Dream, as is college attendance. This is true regardless of the age of the students. Adult students are as motivated as younger ones to attend college for its material benefits instead of its impact on their mental well-being. All students know what they want to be, and that, for most, is simply to be a graduate.

Few colleges turn them away. Instead, most offer students more career-oriented programs, primarily so these institutions can remain competitive in the higher education market. The popular areas of study in colleges have been in the fields perceived to lead to lucrative, high-paying positions such as those in business and engineering. To illustrate, in 1989, 24.5 percent of all freshmen proposed to major in business or management, 10.2 percent in engineering, and only 8.7 percent in the arts and humanities. Sandi Cooper and Dean Savage (1996) have noted that in the past twenty years, the curriculum of the City University of New York (CUNY) has become predominantly vocational. In 1976, York College gave fewer than 10 percent of its degrees in vocational programs; in 1992, over 70 percent of the degrees were in these programs. Vocational degrees from Medgar Evers College increased from 13 to 57 percent of all degrees during the same time period. Apparently, the CUNY administration is convinced that this is what students want; the changes are consumer-driven. This supports a 1980 statement by Arthur Levine that the philosophy of students has changed from "the more you learn, the more your earn" to "the more you learn *of the right things,* the more you earn" (p. 107). Levine concludes that colleges have been eager to offer students more of the right stuff to keep both parties in business.

Conformity

Conformity, not critical thinking, is the product of such academic enterprises, and conformity abounds at many institutions. Joseph Campbell (1988) might argue that colleges are graduating Darth Vaders—unformed people, robots, and bureaucrats—who have not fully developed their own humanity and who live not in terms of themselves but in terms of an imposed system: "This is the threat to our lives that we all face today. Is the system going to flatten you out and deny you your humanity, or are you going to be able to make use of the system to the attainment of human purposes" (p. 144).

Students are natural conformists, even as they struggle to find themselves. Temporary small-group identities antedate long-term individual ones. "Frat rat" is a redundancy, not an oxymoron. Group identity, like group think, is supposed to be a temporary phase in the development of individuals.

Eccentric professors might show students the joy of individuation, but professors are not immune to conformity either, despite their individualistic and sometimes misanthropic images. At any faculty picnic, the professors of music can be discerned easily from the economists, the nursing faculty from the engineers, and the educationists from the physicists.

The evils of superficial appearance are nowhere nearly as great as those of deeper conformist behaviors. Faculty have been encouraged to conform at all levels throughout the history of American higher education. The wealthy benefactors of the early private universities wished to maintain the economic conditions under which they had made their wealth. They looked with disfavor on any faculty member who encouraged social reform. They pressured the universities and withheld money in some cases to silence or remove social reformers from the university. When Professor Edward Bemis was fired by the University of Chicago for his support of the 1894 Pullman strike, university president William Rainey Harper gave a speech about the public work of professors: they were bound to teach a subject, not their opinions. Afterward, Bemis decried the crass commercial spirit of the university. It had established a "line" agreeable to business interests from which no professors could deviate and hope to keep their positions (Hofstadter and Metzger, 1955).

More subtle pressures are offered today when a professor moves too far toward social reform, institutional reform, or even when he or she tries to reform a professional endeavor. The boards of trustees in most institutions are not unlike the boards of review for many professional journals. They govern who gets the rewards of acclaim and eventual remuneration for their efforts. Usually, conservative ideas—those that accept the institution or the canon of the profession as it is—prevail. The exceptions are when institutions or professions are in dire economic and reputational straits. They might be looking for alternative ideas and alternative sources of power. The need to survive supersedes the convenience of conformity.

Consumerism

The student is no longer the product of higher education; he or she is the consumer of it. This notion received legal backing when eighteen-year-olds received the rights of voting citizenship during the Vietnam War. Its logic has been apparent much longer. Thorstein Veblen ([1918] 1957) describes the university of medieval and early modern times as a barbarian university, worldly wise, and given over to the pragmatic, utilitarian disciplines. Virtually every backwoods American colonial college offered more high school–level education than collegiate education. As I stated in Chapter Six, applied subjects were included with the liberal arts, and in most such institutions, they quickly moved from partial or parallel to equal status with their esoteric siblings. The land grant institution was founded later to provide training in the practical arts that was no less valued than training in the liberal ones, and to help politicians appease a public that desired a useful education instead of just a fancy one.

Consumerism goes beyond the curriculum. Enrollment management and other student services are offered so that students will continue to pay tuition. We want these consumers to keep coming back. Lifelong learning and thus lifelong tuitions are a natural extension of consumer satisfaction. But even if the development office is only interested in the financial benefits of keeping students in college, students will grow more by staying there: both profit from increased retention.

Students-as-consumers are paying adults who do not seek to be changed fundamentally by the college environment. Adult consumers shape the nature of an educational experience more than they are shaped by it. This can evoke laissez-faire behaviors on the part of colleges. Not wanting to intrude, they leave their adult consumers alone to choose their experiences. This is especially easy to do on commuter campuses, where individual attendance is restricted to a brief time each day. However, the curriculum at all consumer-driven institutions feeds recognized hungers rather than those not immediately apparent. While this is democratic at one level and assuredly capitalistic at all others, it is only partially educational.

The Bourgeois Virtues

When capitalist values are joined with democratic values, the off-spring is bourgeois virtues that might be uniquely American. Donald McCloskey (1994) says that if we scratch a pro-American, we scratch a bourgeois. He contrasts patrician, plebeian, and bourgeois values. The patrician values of courage, honor, and grace emerge from Mount Olympus, with Achilles as their representative. The plebeian values of duty and service can be found in the Sermon on the Mount. Jesus taught them. The bourgeois values of secular active enterprise have a different patron—the inventor and newspaper man, Benjamin Franklin.

McCloskey writes about bourgeois virtues in the same way that John Dewey wrote about pragmatic truths, confirming the value found in personal experience and social institutions, not in sets of propositions. Bourgeois virtues are local, not universal. They are found uptown and not up in the skies. McCloskey thinks that modern society needs poetry and history and movies that extol all the bourgeois virtues of integrity, honesty, trustworthiness, enterprise, humor, respect, modesty, consideration, responsibility, prudence, thrift, affection, and self-possession. He thinks that these virtues are middle-sized moral values, just as much as those the academy is supposed to represent. If he is right about the nature and source of these values, then the central problem is not with these values but with what happens when they are isolated from a democratic context, in other words from values such as justice, individuation, and community.

The separation of capitalism from democracy is as misguided as any alleged separation of the academy from the real world. John Coleman (1974), former president of Haverford, argues that students are threatened by the latter separation every day. They hear, "Wait till you get into the real world." This view is reinforced by placement officers and commencement speakers: "Now that you are about to enter the real world. . . ." Either way is empty. A campus is no more unreal than a ditch, a restaurant, or a corporate office, and a capitalist enterprise cannot exist fully apart from the values of our nation. The excesses of separation—of too much materialism, narcissism, competition, vocationalism, and consumerism in the academic world can and must be controlled by the social virtues of a democracy.

Altruistic Egoism

The bourgeois weighs the costs and benefits of service against each other to see if the practice is economically worthwhile. The cost of apparent selflessness is the loss of immediate profits. The benefits are that guilt is overcome, pride is enhanced, and satisfied customers keep coming back.

Altruistic egoism is more attainable and sustainable than the selfless service I described in Chapter Two. It serves the server as much as the client. Good service to others guarantees continued and increased use of the products and functions of the service provider. Everybody profits.

Thus, the term *business ethics* is not a complete contradiction. Capitalism does not need to be purely narcissistic or unethical. In fact, McCloskey (1994) contends that bourgeois capitalism is more ethical than either self-satisfied, aristocratic country-club capitalism or self-hating, peasant-like grasping giving. The altruism of the bourgeois might not be the charity of the Bible, but it is reciprocal. Wealth gives back its profits to the poor. To say, "I gave at the office" is required in America.

Enterprise

Overweening competitiveness yields shark-like behaviors. The fittest survive at the expense of all others. But democratic competitiveness boosts all the members of the species. McCloskey writes that more than facts are necessary for successful capitalism. Success depends on enterprise and single-mindedness. No modern bureaucracy is just a rational organization. A business person without an erotic drive, suitably sublimated, achieves nothing.

Intellectual puffery insists otherwise—that reason alone is needed for success, and many intellectuals see businesspeople as the Other, the Enemy, because of their passion for commercial gain (McCloskey, 1994). However, these accusers should look in a mirror before they call other people names. Richard Hofstadter

(1963) distinguishes between true intellectuals and those who use their minds for gain. Professors usually fall into the latter category. Few faculty write because of the joy of the task, but because publication is their one best way to get tenured and promoted. It is easy to debase this type of publishing because it is instrumental and not altruistic and more material than ideational. But even this type of publishing reveals the enterprise of the authors; they are improving themselves and perhaps others.

The value of enterprise is internalized by many doctoral students through the dissertation process. Few examine great ideas, or even cutting-edge topics, for the love of learning about them or for other selfless reasons. They pursue a topic that will be marketable afterward: would-be administrators want to show future employers that they know how to manage; faculty aspirants want to get published. Ben Franklin would be proud of both groups.

It is true that some professors seem to have chosen lives free of any competition as others know the term. Many, soon to retire, are children of the 1960s who rejected the five-goal system of the 1950s: money, power, success, prestige, and security. But unlike other students of their time, these faculty did not reject the concomitant work values of self-discipline, career effort, and achievement, that is, of enterprise. The same holds true for many of their younger colleagues. Good faculty should model enterprise but not excessive competition in their fields and to their students.

Bourgeois Community

Enterprise turns the focus of competitiveness from others to ourselves. Democracy molds enterprise into a sense of community. An example comes from Little League baseball. Coach Larry Rosen (1996) sympathizes with the child who will be forever condemned to play right field, but he rails against the parent who refuses to accept the reason that "it's because [he] couldn't catch the damn ball!" Rosen then lists the following bourgeois virtues of democratic competitiveness: the team matters more than the individual; achievement comes only as a result of adequate preparation; control, perseverance, and calm under pressure are vital elements of character; and constructive criticism is infinitely more valuable than empty praise. These attributes of competitiveness and of enterprise would please any intellectual, as well as any ball player.

Over time, capitalist relationships can become communal. Parties look out for themselves, but they create other relationships that transcend the simplistic purposes of their exchange. A market prospers only when customers are satisfied with the services and products they receive. Responding to Cooper and Savage's criticism of the CUNY system, Arthur Rothkopf (1996), president of Lafayette College, declared that those who argue broadly for liberal arts education must make it clear that they respect the fact that students shopping for colleges have jobs on their minds as well as education, and assure them that the two are compatible. A meeting of the minds can occur, even in the market place.

Conclusion

Pure capitalism seldom exists in the academy. It is modified by the scholarly and democratic values around it. Pure capitalism is like selfless service—seldom attainable or sustainable.

Altruistic service, however, has an additional medium—a pulpit from which to preach its virtues. That medium is the religiously affiliated institution, which Warren Bryan Martin called the "college of character." But even this institution is affected by the capitalist and academic values around it. Religiously affiliated institutions are keenly aware of their market share. They preach Virtues with a capital "V" to a specified audience that will sustain their functioning and thus their purposes. I will describe those purposes next, in a chapter about the spiritual challenges to the values of the academy.

Chapter Eleven

Spirituality: The Challenges of Ultimate Meaning

All human beings must deal with ultimate values as well as the middle-sized ones I describe in this book. Richard Morrill (1981) defines the ultimate values as the universal human phenomenon of faith as a value, faith as an experience of the meaning of life, and faith that life is worth living. Students, faculty, and administrators face the ultimate whenever they question the manner and meaning of their existence, whenever they ask about the good life. Each person needs to matter, and thus each has to deal with values that transcend his or her mortality. William Rogers (1989) includes among these transcendent values, compassion, fidelity, forgiveness, truth seeking, justice, the good of knowledge, and the knowledge of the good.

Spirituality can be wedded to religion or divorced from it. In Allen Withers's (1993) study of private college department chairs, spirituality was associated with Judeo-Christian traditions, spiritual growth, and inner-directedness. For some people, it represented the recognition of a divine being, while others viewed spirituality as refined thinking and feeling about matters of the spirit. All the respondents might have agreed that spirituality involves the third of the great virtues; alongside truth and beauty stands the good.

Grooming the good used to be a daily ritual in American colleges. The character of the student was formed through required courses, academic lectures, daily chapel, and strict codes of conduct. A course on moral philosophy integrated and gave religious purpose to the senior's entire course of study. Graduation depended on the student's Christian comportment as well as his grades. In 1839, more than 80 percent of the presidents of American colleges were clergy, and their esteem as educators depended on the strength of their church connections (Smith, 1956). Religion was so enmeshed in the academy that it could be written that Christian churches did not play a unique role in American higher education—they *were* American higher education (Brauer, 1958). Even today, the ideas of value-oriented higher education survive in the purposes, curriculum, and philosophy of religiously affiliated institutions more than any others (Martin, 1982).

For the past century, public institutions have dominated American higher education to the extent that it is difficult to look at a shirt with "Michigan" or "Wyoming" printed on it and not think of the university as well as the state. The approach to spiritual values is different in public institutions than in private ones. Rights of worship might be protected, but they are not promoted there. The Bible may be taught as a relic of history or a classic of literature but not as a religious document. If religion is taught at all in their courses, students examine it from the outside looking in—from the beliefs to the believers—and all religions are treated with equal superficiality. Any moral directives are filtered from assigned readings or lecture notes, because students are legal adults in these colleges and not moral novitiates. Thus, their spiritual well-being is a by-product instead of a main result of a public college education. When they look up to the stars, students in these colleges will not have heaven pointed out to them.

Irving Kristol (cited in Quie, 1977) contends that a majority of Americans end up holding in contempt all institutions that minimalize spirit. They find these institutions unresponsive to their basic needs and actually repressive. Kristol suggests that educational institutions have come to be regarded as prisons, because they have forsaken their obligation to form students. They have not done enough to consciously help students create a moral identity.

What happened to the psyche of higher education over the past century is more important here than the tangible manifestations of religious concern. Many of the values of religious institutions have been sublimated rather than eliminated. The sacred values of the academy have not disappeared. They have become simpler, secular versions of the absolute, offered up in books like this one that do not discuss morality so much as secular service.

For example, George Marsden (1994) writes that the values of the Protestant establishment are freedom, democracy, benevolence, justice, reform, inclusiveness, brotherhood, and service—most of which have been key values in this book.

In his essay on "knowledge ethics," Clark Kerr (1994) writes that he was startled that academics were very reluctant to deal with ethical issues. He sensed that they wanted to leave those issues to the church because they were matters of personal taste, with one exception—a commitment to scientific truth. One exception would seem to permit an entire discussion, especially since Kerr also notes that many people outside the academy assume that faculty are doing the Lord's work with complete purity and dedication. Kerr includes several pages on the limitations of both the scientific and sacred views of the academy.

This chapter includes the following points. First, differences between academic and spiritual values are both of kind and extension. Second, spirituality evokes the human need for unity and caring, but the integrative, emotional, and universal character of these needs is difficult to reconcile with academic activities today. Third, several of the values of the academy are modified when they are related to spiritual values: service entails sacrifice; the subjective individual becomes moral; so does the community.

In the Essentials, Unity

When parishioners attend the Federated Baptist Church in West Willington, Connecticut, they might pause to read a plaque on the door bearing this comment by Richard Baxter: "In the essentials, unity; in the non-essentials, liberty; and in all things, charity." The statement marks the lines and limits of the spiritual absolute, especially its first and last clauses. Spirituality means unity and universality.

Unity

Spiritual truth appears as illumination. It is revealed in a picture or a parable, not a line of reasoning. Joseph Campbell (1988) considered illumination to be the recognition of the radiance of one eternity through all things. Saints receive it, artists express it, and the rest of us strive for it. However, academics might have a more difficult time finding this unity than others. Campbell writes, "I don't think you get it through sheer academic philosophy, which gets all tangled up in concepts. But just living with one's heart open to others in compassion is a way wide open to all" (p. 163). Spirit is unified, invisible, permanent, and wise instead of fragmented, apparent, temporary, and merely smart.

The central theme in religion and myth is the unity that lies beneath the surface of existence. Life is an illusion. Its real meaning is found in the unseen but experienced unity of us all. The Greeks found unity in reason, that condition of mind that elevated humans above the animals, but they might have been the last academics to feel quite so illuminated. Truth fractured was the topic of Chapter Three. Science has uncovered secular splinters instead of the one spiritual truth that everyone craves.

The invisible nature of such a universal truth makes it impossible to detect through scientific means. Observing the invisible is not an easy task, whether empiricists are looking for a black hole or the human soul. It cannot be observed even if it can be experienced, nor do its "facts" lead to verifiable conclusions. It cannot be proven that hammers should be used for bludgeoning nails instead of humans, even though most people know they should be.

Spiritual truth must stand the test of time. A classic is included in the St. John's curriculum only if it contains wisdom, illumination, and understanding. The criteria do not include scientific experiment or facts nouveau. Spiritual truth rarely jumps out at an observer; it percolates into a person's consciousness, with brewed character.

The essentials are true, but even more, they are wise. The elevation of wisdom over scientific truth is apparent in the lines of Whitman's poem "When I Heard the Learned Astronomer." The student [grown tired and sick from all the proofs, charts, diagrams, and lecturing of the astronomer], wanders off by himself in the mystical moist night air, and from time to time, looks up in perfect silence at the stars. Academic science expands knowledge, but the wisdom of how to use knowledge lies largely beyond the scope of science. It requires truth fused by spirit and implemented as moral action. This was the original purpose of moral philosophy that saw no separation of science from spirit. Its progeny, the social sciences, see no integration of science with spirit.

Theodore Hesburgh (1979) acknowledges that education is essentially concerned with the intellect, the formation of intelligence, and the search for knowledge. But he also writes that educators must be concerned with values, because "wisdom is more than knowledge, man is more than his mind, and without values, man may be intelligent but less than fully human" (p. xi).

Liberty

When doubt became the basic motivation for science, science and spirit parted company. Doubt creates plural possibilities that do not stop with secular matters. They extend to every essential. Abundant doubts appear to be the arch-enemies of absolute faith.

Members of the "religious right" in the United States believe that a theology of doubt has replaced God in most schools and colleges. They label independent thinking as secular humanism, which evangelist Jimmy Swaggart claimed was destroying the home; Jerry Falwell considered it to be Satan, and Tim LaHaye called it atheistic amoral depravity (Park, 1987). These ministers reacted in anger instead of agony about the loss of first principles in the academy.

It is difficult to determine, much less reach consensus about, the precise point at which nonessentials are indoctrinated and essentials are pluralized to the detriment of either. This assessment has affected the teaching of any subject that involves ethics in today's academy. In public schools, only secular values can be taught. The Lemon Test is the product of a 1971 U.S. Supreme Court case concerning the constitutionality of school values programs. It involves three steps. First, the program must have a secular purpose. Second, it must have a principal or primary effect of neither advancing nor inhibiting religion. Finally, it must not foster excessive government entanglement with religion (Amundson, 1991).

Some might contend that the academy has joined public schools in the development of a form of "inclusive" higher education that resolves the problems of pluralism by excluding all religious perspectives within it. This phenomenon began during the 1880s and continues to this day. In contrast, many religious groups have pursued the opposite strategy. They have excluded all diversity, and some have homogenized their practices in order to appeal to the broadest clientele.

Pluralism is either an objective observation or a normative value. It can be observed that we live in a society with a wide range of values and behaviors that are often in conflict. However, within that society there is also a normative belief in freedom and individuation. The diversity of people and values is valued beyond their unity (Hastings Center, 1980). The latter position seems prominent in most public universities today. These are the bastions of research science, empirical truth, and perhaps a consequent belief: "In All Things, Liberty."

Charity

The Baxter statement was written in 1510, and "charity" is translated from the Latin term *caritas,* meaning basic love more than sympathetic devotion. The caring spirit is universal and ultimate. Teilhard de Chardin, the French theologian and paleontologist, considered such love to be more important than harnessing the winds and waves. It was humanity's second discovery of fire.

Universalism

I discussed moral equality in Chapter Five and the plebeian nature of spiritual values in Chapter Ten. Every man, woman, and child has equal moral potential.

Everyone is admitted to the spiritual institution, and grades are distributed according to good actions, not mental prowess. This point is illustrated in Graham Greene's (1982) modern rendition of the story of Don Quixote. Quixote, a parish priest, travels through Spain and talks about religion with Sancho, now a Communist. He confesses that the fine points of moral theology confuse him, because Quixote is an ignorant man. All he really knows is found in the books of the saints. They wrote of love, and Quixote understands love. The other things do not seem quite so important to him.

The Emotion of Love

The Dalai Lama said that it is more important than ever before that universities shoulder the responsibility of developing good hearts as well as able brains. He noted that knowledge is an instrument, and human affection makes for the constructive use of knowledge. Education can foster self-discipline if it teaches concern for others' rights and close feelings toward others (Woodford, 1994). In the choice of head or heart, the heart prevails in the spiritual institution.

During the 1960s, the value of universal love was associated with hippies, but it was also washed, rinsed, and ironed into respectability by humanistic psychologists. No matter the number of launderings, however, no emotion is ever worn easily by academicians who consider themselves to be, above all, thinking men and women. Love is not just the subjective inexplicable to them, it is anti-intellectual and interferes with their work. Love and spirituality are expressed through poetry, pictures, and individual acts, which the intellectual sees as clumsy approximations of truth. The advocate of spirit agrees that these manifestations of love are penultimate expressions of truth, because the ultimate cannot be put into words (Campbell, 1988).

Some defenders of the spirit offer a none-too-loving response to the advocates of intellect. Evangelicals have been some of the most powerful opponents of intellectualism, especially in America, which has been shaped by an evangelical spirit. The religious right is a powerful political as well as religious group that hates the habitual heresy of intellectuals and disputes the basic tenets of modern science—that evidence, rationality, and thoughtful analysis are more important than convenient dogmatism (Brandt, 1987).

Any name-calling belies the fact that emotions and spirit have been separated from the discovery and study of knowledge only during the past century. Richard Hofstadter (1963) has written that it is pointless to divorce intellect from all the other human qualities with which it can be combined. Intellect does not stand against the other human excellences but as a complement to them, without which all cannot be fully consummated. Mind is a guide to emotion, not a guarantee of character. David Patterson titled a 1996 book, *When Learned Men Murder,* in order to underline the need for academies to teach and model moral behavior. There are no guarantees, but universal love is at least one guide to knowledge, unsatisfied until ideas make good.

At least one of the great methods of reasoning—deduction—is as important to epistemology as it is to theology. Specific knowledge descends from absolute principles. Whether or not God sends this knowledge down to humanity might be a different issue than whether or not the spirit and its attendant absolutes deserve academic attention.

The passion of arguments about intellect and emotion attests to the presence of love in the learning community. The devotion of the academic to learning is at least as passionate and sacred as the devotion of the cleric to God. Each devotion entails a special sense of the ultimate. Parker Palmer (1987) agrees that the learning community is held together by its love of learning and its love of learners. He considers this love to be spiritual as well as passionate. Mutual empowerment requires all the love—as well as the skill—that the community of teaching and learning has to offer.

Modifying Service, Individuation, and Community

Spirit should affect a person's perception of all the values of the academy because spirit involves the ultimate. Truth, freedom, justice, service, community, individuation, and equality—all become great values when spirit is intertwined with them. Sans spirit, sans greatness. However, this review focuses on three of the values—service, individuation, and community. Nuances of meaning are more important here than absolute distinctions between academic and ultimate values.

The choice of these three values comes from a review of the values at five Catholic colleges and universities (Murphy, 1990). After surveying faculty, students, and alumni, Barry University uncovered four core values: a caring environment, respect for the person, service to the underprivileged, and high academic standards. The core values of Trinity College in Vermont were caring or making the human connection, a family community, a personal challenge, and respect for the individual. St. Mary of the Woods College in Indiana identified academic excellence, social concern, community, and tradition. The core values of Santa Clara University in California were academic excellence, educating the whole person, public service, and a spirit of community and worship. Finally, DePaul University in Chicago put its core values into three categories: academic quality, teaching and academic freedom; religious personalism, including respect for the individual and human dignity; and an urban characteristic that values diversity and attempts to serve the underprivileged. The values of service, individuation, and community are emphasized in the core values of these religiously affiliated institutions, thus, they will be the focus of this discussion.

Service as Sacrifice

John Gardner (1961) writes that spiritual people place themselves at the service of values that transcend their own individuality, the values of professions and cultures and, above all, the religious and moral values that nourish the ideal of individual fulfillment in the first place. But this service wins our admiration only if the act of giving does not cripple the individuality that motivates it: "We cannot admire faceless, mindless servants of The State or The Cause or The Organization who were never mature individuals and who have sacrificed all individuality to the Corporate Good" (p. 137).

Religious service differs from academic service and, even more, from bourgeois reciprocity or capitalistic greed. Religious service comes without any sense of reward, and usually it requires the sacrifice of one's earthly interests in order to serve others. This sacrifice might involve the loss of property or life. Some cynics might say, "Sure, but the purpose is to earn the reward of heaven," thus making spiritual service more opportunistic than even capitalistic greed. But such a reward sought is never supposed to be attained, and even if one achieves a spot in heaven, it seems to be the ultimate in delayed gratification. The value of purely selfless service is, essentially, morality carried to its logical conclusion. Its symbol is the martyr. Few chief executive officers need apply.

Moral Subjectivity

John Gardner's comments link individuality with spirituality. The true individual is a moral actor, not a rational object. Objectivism violates the subjective reality of the person, but the measure of meaning in the academy has been through objectivism and its partners—impersonalism, instrumentalism, specialization, reductionism, atomism, and amorality (Rogers, 1989). Parker Palmer (1987) writes that "this seemingly abstract way of knowing, this seemingly bloodless epistemology becomes an ethic. It is an ethic of competitive individualism in the midst of a world fragmented and made exploitable by that very mode of knowing" (p. 22). Students become trained schizophrenics. They are taught about a world out there somewhere apart from them, divorced from their lives, instead of experienced. Students educated without transcendent values suffer from excessive anxiety about economic issues, narcissism, and a resulting focus on personal issues, and anomie—the loss of a believable center of experience (Rogers, 1989). Such students are spiritually restless, and the university offers them no place to call home. They seek that personal transformation that science has denied them. They seek a spiritual awakening of their subjective uniqueness.

Warren Bryan Martin (1982) dedicated the title and theme of his book about independent colleges, *The College of Character,* to an essay by Martin Buber (1965) entitled, "The Education of Character." In that essay, Buber links spiritual unity to the development of individuals who are responsible for themselves and others. Ethical character is an attitude that, in action, prefers absolute values before all others. The unity of the person and of the lived life has to be emphasized again and again. It must not yield to the confusing contradictions of the collective. Buber wrote that educators must develop character by example instead of by lecture. The I-Thou relationship is a dialogue, not a monologue. The educator who helps any person fulfill the unity inherent in a responsible life will help put that person face-to-face with God.

Science and technology have made people collectively powerful but individually weak. Objectivism means an empty life or worse, a life of distorted subjectivity, that is, an immoral one. Just as Martin Buber distinguished between I-Thou and I-It relationships, the spirit of humanity is discovered in the moral relationships among subjective beings, not in their commercial or mental transactions. This spiritual subjectivity is a root of the political philosophy that founded the nation. It stands above the commerce of enterprise and the science of the academy. Moral subjectivity is personified by the religious savior, who models the fulfilled human being in relationship to others. In the colonial colleges, the president took on this role as abbot of the college, and later, the dean assumed some of these specific roles. An early dean said his job was helping people to do things difficult enough to cut lines in their souls.

The Moral Community

The value of community is organic and natural. Community is the social outcome of natural law and, therefore, an entity of spirit more than mind. The organic community does not have to overthrow objectivity, analysis, and experimentation in order to do its work, but it must put them into a context affirming the communal nature of reality itself—the *relational* nature of reality (Palmer, 1987). After acknowledging the prevalence of pluralism, it is important to find a moral and benevolent meeting ground (Rogers, 1989).

The spiritual community deals with moral justice. No single individual determines this justice; the assemblage does. The terrible swift sword of the community will do its duty, which means more to the assemblage than merely being fair to others. In the best circumstances, the spirit of moral community is expressed through social service. In the worst, the success of the Fighting Irish depends on their ability to kill the Bloody Brits, instead of their ability to defeat some Boilermakers at football.

Ritual and Conformity

The spiritual community makes its members participate in rituals that demonstrate their acceptance of the group standard and their forfeiture of some individual needs. The goal of such collective behavior is not the mere empowerment of individuals but the empowerment of a higher spirit through the individual. Robert Fulghum (1995) says that ritual refers to two kinds of acts: those things we do for the first time that in fact have been done by the human race forever, and those things we repeat again and again because they bring structure to our individual and collective lives. Ritual is easy when it involves attendance at a football game or at graduation exercises. It is meaningful when the individual wants to participate in it. At other times, ritual involves meaningless conformity to group standards.

H. L. Mencken said that his objection to Puritans was not that they try to make us think as they do, but that they try to make us do as they think. Mencken also defined conscience as the inner voice that warns us that someone else is looking and self-respect as the secure feeling that no one, as yet, is suspicious. While laughing at the cynicism of these comments, many people will look over their shoulders to see who is watching them, because of the pressures of conformity. Denominational colleges demand more social propriety than public institutions, but conformity is not confined to these institutions. In capitalistic enterprises, similar conformity can be demanded for a different reward—financial empowerment.

The excesses of religious conformity are familiar to campuses that have dealt with cults. Some of the "true believers" have used a little learning and a lot of oppression to recruit student members. They have reinforced the affiliative needs of students while suppressing their emerging individuality. They have hated reason and the people who love it, because reason is divorced from the faith they demand. The academy is opposed to God. Kant was more of a subversive than Robespierre. The Frenchman only executed a king, while the German killed God with his *Critique of Pure Reason* (Harrington, 1983).

Conclusion

Reckoning with the ultimate is not just a job for philosophers, scientists, or any other academic specialists. It is a task for every person on campus and off. The formal responsibilities of that task can be examined and perhaps defined, but they can never be proscribed. Spiritual unity and love are universal needs, and thus, they cannot be placed within a sector of the academy. Ultimately, all education has to deal with some comprehension of the ultimate.

In the next chapter, I discuss another ultimate value—beauty—which is expressed and appreciated through aesthetics. Both spirituality and aesthetics represent challenger values to academic values, and perhaps even more to capitalism. Spirituality and aesthetics challenge each other as well, because art is not necessarily moral, though it must be profound. In discussing the career of Derek Walcott, who won the Nobel Prize for Literature, Anne Bernays (1993) compares his reputation as a harasser of young women to his poetry. She declares that his poetry was one thing, his life was something else. "Pity they don't match, but there it is. Some of the most sublime works have been turned out by people you wouldn't dream of shaking hands with" (p. B1).

Chapter Twelve

Aesthetics: The Challenges of Linking Emotion with Intellect

In an interview in *Down Beat* magazine, pianist Keith Jarrett (Eph-land, 1996) talked about the completeness of a jazz trio. He said, three is a strong number. It is positive, negative, and neutral. It is pro, con, and mediator. Otherwise, everything falls apart. As for the musicians in his own trio, Jarrett stated that he is a coldhearted social critic, the drummer a warmhearted optimist, and the bassist a research scientist. After the laughter died down, Jack DeJohnette, the drummer, responded, "Yeah, but somewhere, when we play, though, all that goes out the window. There's a point where the music takes us" (p. 18).

I have stated throughout this text that philosophy has its own strong trio of truth, good, and beauty. Each has a distinct sound, and each is played a different way. All three are needed to make a life music instead of chaotic noise. Truth is the piano in this particular etude, and good sneaks its beat into any discussion about values, but beauty seems out of tune with the other instruments. To this point, she has not been plucked, thumped, or bowed, perhaps because her role in this piece is so uncertain.

Aesthetics is neither spirit nor science, ethics nor logic, and it is difficult to describe exactly what it is. Aesthetics involves the perception and expression of art. Perceived beauty can be explained simply, as whatever the eye beholds, or complexly, through the terms of a science of symbolic expression. Either way, it is easier to explain beauty than to create it. True art is created freehand. It is not drawn within someone else's lines. Norman MacLean (1976) writes that all good things—trout fishing as well as eternal salvation—come by grace, and grace comes by art, and art does not come easy. Aesthetics is hard work without smoothness, what John Brubacher (1965) calls the "stubborn interaction between the artist and a medium" (p. 44). Its relationship with the academy is more abrasive than soothing.

I offer the following points in this chapter. First, professors dismiss aesthetics because it seems illogical, but aesthetic truth integrates emotion and intellect. Second, aesthetic properties of harmony, symbolization, emotion, intuitive vision, and unity are important additions to our conception of scientific truth. Third, aesthetics lived is individuation fulfilled. Students are art, original and irreplaceable. Their emotional depth and creativity must be nurtured by the academy. Fourth, the development of artistry requires more than hedonistic indulgence, emphasis on the material, and comfortable conformity. Finally, aesthetics might be the least controversial of the new paradigms that challenge traditional science. It provides a common ground for the seekers of alternative truths.

Dismissing the Importance of Aesthetics

Because we do not understand its identity very well, it seems easy to dismiss aesthetics as an essential value of the academy. Kenneth Benne ([1948] 1962) writes that aesthetics is always criticized by "Philistines," "Professors," "and Puritans" (p. 469). The Philistine says that the arts bake no bread, they meet no payrolls, and they make no direct contribution to the practical, pecuniary life of our economy. Aesthetics is not a material value, and this is above all a material world. Professors are positivists. They correlate the growth of intelligence with the method of science; therefore, aesthetics is superseded by scientific analysis and specialized inquiry. A thing of beauty might be a joy forever, but that will not suffice. Joy must be defined and the thing dissected in order for an academician to smile. Puritans say that the arts are decadent. They are pleasurable, and anything that makes a person happy is immoral. The Puritans might think that every night is Saturday night in a campus residence hall. They have evidence to point to, those prodigal students who argue that purple hair, excessive drinking, and destructive sex are part of their self-exploration, their self-discovery, and their artistic right to destroy themselves. The Prodigals try to turn every night into Saturday night in the residence halls.

The effeteness of art for art's sake, the anti-intellectualism of art for emotion's sake, and the hedonism of art for pleasure's sake make the value of aesthetics easy to dismiss. Even in that bastion of general education—the liberal arts college—faculty, department chairs, and cabinet administrators rank aesthetics as their lowest work value, raising great doubts about its rank in the remainder of higher education (Skaggs, 1987; Withers, 1993; Morris, 1994).

Yet aesthetics does not go away. Some quite proper people embrace it. Through art exhibits in the union, dance troupes in the theater, general courses, and college publications, administrators and faculty try to get people to appreciate beauty. Students learn about the fine arts as well as the most popular ones in order to build their aesthetic experiences and perceptual capacities. Joseph Ben-David (1972) asserts that the central purpose of general education is to make students aesthetically superior to others. Not just reason, but the appreciation of beauty elevates human beings above anthropoid apes; the Greeks would have liked that notion. And the college viewbook might convince some applicants to enroll if they think the campus is pretty. Many a Philistine would like that one.

Aesthetics refracts at least and illuminates at best the other values of the academy. This discussion focuses on the relationship of aesthetics to the values of truth and individuation.

Aesthetic Truth

Like its sister, spirituality, aesthetic truth does not support simple scientific truth, at least not if intellect is totally separated from emotions. Aesthetic truth is more integrative than that; it organizes the animism of life. Robert Hutchins (1949) believed that the primary role of higher education is intellectual and not moral. However, he did not exclude the Muse from intellectual pursuits. He perceived that intellect is rooted in philosophy, in principles of "why," which are not posed or answered by rationalistic science. The whys of humanity are revealed in music, art, and literature as well as philosophy—in aesthetics.

Aesthetic truth is lyrical more than linear, and its elements contrast with some of the elements of empirical science. They include harmony, symbolization, emotion, intuition, and unity. Their scientific counterparts are linearity, facts, reason, and fragmentation.

Harmony

Harmony involves density and repleteness, the proportion and pattern of a work of art. Density means the number and order of symbols within a scheme, and repleteness concerns the comprehensiveness of features in a scheme (Goodman, 1980). These are holistic components, not linear attributes, but they are not irrelevant to science. The Dancing Wu Li Masters (Zukav, 1990) define physics as patterns of organic energy. This definition leads Gary Zukav to the conclusion that scientists, poets, painters, and writers are all in the same family. They take the ordinary and then represent it in ways that enlighten us.

Density is the number and arrangement of symbols in a work of art, to be found, for example, in the arrangement of faculty offices in any academic department. Perhaps the full professors have the only offices with windows. The assistant professors have smaller rooms near the dean's office. The emeriti professors have offices near the doors, and the graduate assistants share one office next to the copying machine. The location and density of offices reveals a department's perception of faculty rank.

Repleteness shows that the picture is complete. Driving around some campuses reveals their incompleteness as pictures. Something might be missing from the north end of a campus, perhaps a historical marker where the first building was located. A basketball court might complete the south end of campus. The south end lacks a place for students to play, near the residence halls.

Matisse said that the whole arrangement of his picture was expressive, the place occupied by figures or objects, the empty spaces around them, and the proportions. Everything played a part. Harmony concerns the connections of objects across space, not objects just abutting. A mass of notes does not make music. Instead, music is notes and spaces, properly arranged.

Details are important to harmony too, but they are important because of their ability to reveal the whole of the music. Writing about a choral rehearsal, Bernard Holland (1996) notes that Robert Shaw would make two hundred people sing wrong notes, sing with numbers, add syllables, face each other, and march in time. The consistent message of this madness was that the *spirit* of the music was unintelligible unless the details spoke. The details lay in layers: the right notes, the right tone color, the right meter, the right rhythm, the right words said in the right way. Shaw could isolate and exaggerate each element and then return the elements to their harmonious order.

Symbolization

Symbolization is the metaphoric strength of the canvas. Every campus has its symbols, those buildings and spaces that mean more than concrete and grass. The residence halls provide many examples. Every campus has its "jungle" or "geek house" and every student has a nickname for Fred's, Debbie's, or Abdulla's room. The informal names for and within the residence halls tell more about the art of a campus than the formal names above the doors.

Symbolization extends to entire institutions. The name Kent State signifies an era and an anger many years after the students were shot there. The symbolic wounds of Kent are also felt at Jackson State. Other institutions never escape their vocational or party school images, while still others celebrate the symbolic appearance of their academic strength long after its reality has eroded. These symbolic institutions, their buildings, wings within those buildings, and rooms within those wings reveal the identity of every campus to its students and staff.

Emotion Framed

In Sanskrit, the word *rasa* means the mood or sentiment that is evoked by a work of art. Literally, it refers to the essential oils of a fruit or the perfume of a flower. It is used to capture the emotional essence of art when other words are inadequate (Rheingold, 1988). Nelson Goodman (1980) says that the distinction between the scientific and the aesthetic is somehow rooted in the difference between knowing and feeling; it is the difference between the cognitive and the emotive.

However, aesthetics is more than raw emotion, it is emotion framed. In aesthetic experience, emotions are felt, then cognition discriminates and relates them in order to gauge the work, to grasp it, and to integrate it with the rest of experience (Goodman, 1980). The satisfaction is integrated and organized and not merely indulged. As T. S. Eliot said, the poet expresses the emotional equivalent of thought. The result of that expression is a unity unachievable without aesthetic sensibilities. Perhaps that is the reason Emily Dickinson said that beauty and truth were brethren, they were kinsmen, and John Keats claimed that they were one and the same.

Intuitive Vision

Benedetto Croce (1921) summarizes his opinions about aesthetics in the simplest manner—that art is vision or intuition. *Vision* is a term overworked in popular management primers but seldom related to aesthetics, which has always tried to turn what is in front of our eyes into something new. Vision as artistic intuition is connected to emotion as much as intellect. It is the third part of the mind that links the primitive brain (emotions) with the conscious mind. "Hence, most creative discoveries are intuitively derived and only later 'dressed up' by logic, observation, or some other conscious technique" (Lewis, 1990, p. 138). Aesthetic vision begins with emotions, in all their depth and their breadth, and then uses intellect to organize them. It is not just passionate, it is passionate cognition.

Scientific truth is caught up in reductionist facts and forms. It is difficult to induce vision from unrelated specializations, even if they look like mountains. Aesthetics brings the sky into the landscape. A story has circulated about a man who moved from the Canadian Rockies to central Illinois to get his doctorate at the University of Illinois. "What a beautiful country!" he exclaimed. A native said, "Why do you call this flat, monotonous country beautiful, when you've lived so long in the mountains of Canada?" The man responded, "Oh, you can see so far here. Where I came from, you couldn't see beyond a one-acre patch." Aesthetic vision sees how things should fall together: the picture with the proper density, repleteness, and symbolization; the picture that transcends the one-acre patch.

Unity

The integrative nature of aesthetics has been alluded to earlier. Harmony arranges diverse elements to reveal the invisible unity of the picture. Krishnamurti (1985) says that beauty is unity, and ugliness is fragmentation. As I noted in the chapter on spirituality, unity seems to be a concept of nature but not modern science. It is the aesthetic Muse or religious Spirit that integrates parts into wholes: morality, thought, feeling, and action into wisdom; parents and children into families; arts and sciences into knowledge. Modern science breaks wholes into parts. It fosters understanding through visible, intelligible units and not through invisible unity.

Logic might be informed, true, and linearly complete. Aesthetics adds unity, complexity, elevation, emotions, and imagination to logic to make it whole (Shoemaker, 1943). This might be the fundamental reason why general education includes aesthetic appreciations—they are the last living kin of the rationalist notion that knowledge is unified and whole. William Stott (1983) writes that the purpose of aesthetics is to integrate, synthesize, and correct the kinds of reductive specialization that work against the aims of the liberal arts. To Stott, aesthetics speaks of the beauty and coherence of a realized ideal.

James Joyce related aesthetic harmony to this unity of the ideal. He considered the aesthetic experience to be involved neither with possession nor criticism of an object. It was a simple beholding of the object. It was seen first as one thing, and then its relationships became clear, each part to the whole, and the whole to each of its parts. Joseph Campbell (1988) writes, "This is the essential aesthetic factor—rhythm, the harmonious rhythm of relationships. And when a fortunate rhythm has been struck by the artist, you experience a radiance. You are held in aesthetic arrest. That is the epiphany" (p. 220). The aesthetic epiphany is similar to the religious epiphany, even if it is found first in harmony and then in unity, and not the other way around.

The Artistry of Individuation

It is easier to describe aesthetic truth than to live one's art. Degas noted that painting was not very difficult when one did not know how to paint. But when one knew, then it was a different matter. Art expressed is not replicable; it is individual beauty created. The French leader, François Mitterand, was an artist of himself. Shortly after Mitterand died, William Pfaff (1996) wrote that he was one of those remarkable men who are fundamentally artists, but with themselves and their careers the subject of their art. "He was like a painter in constructing his career, rubbing out the mistakes as he went, shifting the perspective as his vision shifted, always with the final creation in his mind: the completed image that would remain and prevail when he was finished" (p. 41).

Aesthetics lived is individuation fulfilled. Students and faculty and campuses become art. This ambition to individuality pleases, but the outcome is still a concern to Philistines, Puritans, and Professors. Is this person the one described in the chapters on individuation and spirituality, or is this a Prodigal only, whom we are better off without?

Students as Art

Students as art are individuals in an aesthetic context. Annie Dillard (1982) writes that art objects have in them "qualities in which the great world and its parts seem wanting: human significance, human order, reason, mind, causality, boundary, harmony, perfection, coherence, purity, purpose, and permanence" (p. 144)—but only if the viewer considers the world as a text, as a meaningful, purposefully fashioned creation, as a work of art. Emotional vitality, emotional management, and creative imagination are among the most important attributes of the student as art.

Aesthetics does not merely organize feelings, it enlarges them. Our range and depth of feelings might be as distinctively a human characteristic as our intellect. De Unamuno (1963) believed that emotions were our most important attribute and, thus, the most important concern of philosophy. He argued that he had seen a cat reason more often than it laughed or wept. Perhaps it laughed or wept inwardly but then, he reasoned, perhaps the crab, also inwardly, resolved mathematical equations.

Emotional management involves not only the emotions but the identity of the student, his or her feeling of competence, and his or her ability to be autonomous. Aesthetics concerns an individual's full emotional development and his or her subsequent organization of those emotions.

Aesthetics also frees the creative spirit. Robert Henri (1923) writes that the artist is searching, daring, inventive, and self-expressive. Where those who are not artists are trying to close the book, the artist opens it and shows there are still more pages possible.

General education attempts to build creative imagination, which many educators embrace as higher-order thinking. Such thinking is necessary whether the thinkers are students, professors, or administrators. Donald Schön (1987) writes that real professionals know how to solve real-world problems that do not present themselves as well-formed structures. These problems can be framed, but not through classroom theories. The solutions require more improvisation than such theory allows. They must be *created.* Schön might label professionals as values artists. They draw best when there are no lines to color in.

The uniqueness of students gets lost when they are considered only as enrollment data or cultural groups. Students become reproductions, just as Mona Lisas are reproducible on tee-shirts. The context and meaning of the original gets lost. The reproduced image has little or nothing to do with a painting's original independent meaning (Berger, 1972). The preeminent educational value of the academy is the growth of human dignity, here called individuation. The student has importance as an original work of art, not just as one of many reproductions.

The Corruption of Individual Artistry

However, some people use the name of art to indulge themselves. The easy satisfactions of hedonism are substituted for the difficult ones of true beauty. Material possession replaces artistic creation. Creative isolation is avoided, and conformity—even to a rebellious image—replaces the challenge of developing selfhood.

Hedonism

Art involves satisfaction, and that often involves the pleasure principle. Some Puritans find hedonism in any pleasure and abundant examples of hedonism on every college campus, for example, intemperate drinking, graffiti, and date rape. Hunter Lewis (1990) is not the only person who places the aesthete among such advocates of prodigal values as the naïf, the escapist, the profligate, and the decadent.

The satisfactions of art are more than pleasure, however. The tragedies of Shakespeare, the art of Edvard Munch, and the poetry of A. E. Housman are filled with despair. The discomfort of art is part of its essence. Anne Bernays (1993) writes that lasting art is neither polite nor charming. It achieves its effect by taking reality to its limits, by agitating the calm. Whether you "like" it or not is irrelevant. In many nations, the artist is also the activist. The names Solzhenitsyn and Brodsky remind us of the peril of honest artistry in a politically unsavory climate. Even in America, prison art disturbs the viewer sitting at home, because its vision was hatched in the cellblock instead of a sunny atelier.

Many of the satisfactions of beauty are neither pleasurable nor sensate, but just as surely many are, and not all such pleasures should be avoided. Aristotle held that the *summum bonum*—the greatest good—was happiness that was revealed in its highest form through contemplation. He contemplated often the distinction between "difficult beauty" and sheer ugliness.

Aesthetics helps build happiness in a world that smiles too seldom. It reminds administrators to make campuses pleasing places to work and study. It reminds faculty that their courses can be enjoyable as well as challenging. It reminds students that their rooms should be more than just bedrooms, they should be places that are pleasing to live in.

Materialism

Artists differ from art collectors. Art requires a tangible expression of the artist, but the artist does not own the art created. The collector owns it. The artist's image is an aspiration and a representation, but it is not a possession. The artist must be fulfilled by the expressive endeavor instead of its outcome. Owning cool clothes, hot wheels, or a long résumé is less important than creating one's self.

Isolation

Isolation scares some members of the academy, while others relish it. In an essay on the creative process, James Baldwin (1985) writes that the primary distinction of artists is that they actively cultivate the state that most people try to avoid— the state of being alone. Most people are, essentially, alone, but Baldwin believed that artists are compelled to linger with the knowledge of their aloneness. In such a state, they are not part of the active world, but that is not their primary duty. The precise role of the artist is to illuminate the darkness of isolation and to connect it to the rest of the world. The purpose, then, of artistic isolation is to use it to create a more humane community. Isolation is a means, not an end of aesthetic activity.

Conformity

As I stated in Chapter Five, *uni*formity is too low a goal for higher education. However, *con*formity is a purpose of schools and capitalistic enterprises that is, perforce, carried into college. Students are socialized for citizenship and vocational participation. College helps them adapt even more successfully to the social system. James Van Patten (1967) writes that conformity has several virtues: it brings order out of chaos, it enables society and civilization to function, and it gives people security. But a collective will should never smother the creativity of an individual soul.

Aesthetics challenges the order. Leonardo was more an artist than an engineer. A huge rubber stamp sits near the Federal Building in Cleveland, a sculpture by Claus Oldenburg. On the bottom of the stamp is one word, "free." Because this sculpture is such a powerful piece of art, it does not sit next to the British Petroleum building, whose board of directors commissioned it. It was moved out of the ordinary line of sight of Clevelanders, next to the lake, and surprisingly, next to a building run by the greatest bureaucracy in the world. Even there, it is a powerful statement about conformity.

Aesthetics also embraces the quality that conformity fears most—failure. Artistry requires failure. Education avoids it. Charles Kettering liked to differentiate the inventor from the student. The inventor failed ninety-nine times to succeed once, while the student succeeded ninety-nine times to avoid one failure.

Paradigms

Aesthetic perceptions differ from scientific ones. This, more than any other characteristic, has diminished the status of aesthetics within the academy. W. H. Cowley (1961) states that colleges and universities, more than any other Western institutions, uphold the values of science, meaning the values of analytic knowledge. He distinguishes analytic knowledge from poetic knowledge, that is, the knowledge gained through imaginative thinking, intuition, revelation, or other nonanalytic means. Poetic knowledge is "anti-intellectual." It might be acceptable in the domain of poets and clerics but not that of professors. Cowley cites the damnation of science by poets, professors of literature, painters, and others, and he alleges that their anti-intellectualism has slowed the acceptance of the fine arts in the academy more than any vestiges of Puritanism. However, Cowley seems to believe that aesthetics has been as important as science to colleges and universities, though these currents of modern thought continue to flow separately, side by side, rarely finding the same channels.

Paradigm is a thirty-year-old term for different ways of knowing—traditional and emergent, male and female, European and African, and left-brained and right-brained. These might also be labeled scientific and aesthetic ways of knowing. The traditional, male, European, left-brained, and scientific model is linear; information flows in one direction. The emergent, female, African, right-brained, and aesthetic model is multidirectional; information comes from many different directions. The scientific model is objective; people stand outside information that they study. The aesthetic model is subjective; the perceiver affects the phenomenon that is studied. The scientific, masculine, European, and left-brained modes focus on independence, while the aesthetic, feminist, African, and right-brained modes of inquiry focus on context. In sum, the scientific model is mechanistic, and the aesthetic model is organic; the whole is more than the sum of the parts.

It seems unfortunate that aesthetics has rarely been named as one of the forms of alternative thinking. For all its emotionality, aesthetics evokes less passionate dispute than some of the other labels that are attached to contextual cognition. It is just as much at home with women's ways of knowing as feminist paradigms; it preaches cultural diversity at least as well as Afrocentrism; and it has been a stepchild of the academy longer than these colleagues. Aesthetics might be disliked by certain Professors, but aesthetics has never been shut out of the curriculum.

Aesthetics provides a common ground where diverse forms of inquiry might meet: in student centers, residence halls, and classrooms. It is not tainted by identification with any particular cultural group or with any single sex: aesthetics belongs to everyone. It celebrates cultural diversity by celebrating the beauty of diverse clothing, the food, the dances, the crafts, and the "different voices" of different people. Exposure to aesthetics advances alternative ways of thinking, as well as the satisfactions that can come from encountering diversity.

Even science is beginning to accept the importance of art. Authors such as Fritjof Capra (1975) have described the limitations of classical inquiry and the new acceptance of holism, subjective perceptions, and intuitive understandings by modern science. Space and time are inseparable. One cannot be considered without the other. The perceiver has become part of the scientific phenomenon.

Science is getting subjective. It is coming to mean the unresting endeavor and progressive development continually toward an aim that the poetic intuition may apprehend but the intellect can never fully grasp (Plank, cited in Zukav, 1990). Eventually, aesthetics might become a synonym for accurate science. Today, it is an alternative to the limits of logical positivism in the scientific community.

Conclusion

The essence of aesthetics lies in its integration of emotion and intellect and, thence, its enhancement of human dignity. Aesthetics confirms subjective participation in the cognitive process. It requires engagement and then inquiry. Aesthetics enables individuals to develop their emotional depth. It enhances the understanding of cultural diversity. It provides an alternative philosophy to positivist science.

Aesthetics contributes to the essential nature of the academy because it challenges more popular values. However, it is not visible enough. In a recent story in the *New Yorker,* Mark Danner (1996) writes about Hassiba Boulmerka, the runner who was denounced by many Muslims for "running with naked leg in front of thousands of men" while winning the 1,500-meter race at Barcelona. Danner noted that the Greeks had equated excellence with beauty. While some forms of reverence may demand that beauty be covered, here excellence demanded it be revealed. The Greeks would have understood.

Chapter Thirteen

Relating the Values to Changing Times

In this chapter, I discuss the relationships between the academic values and their challengers, addressing the notion of gravitation, the attraction of all bodies of matter—or values—to each other. The values of the academy exist somewhere between those of capitalism on one side and the ultimate values of spirituality and aesthetics on another. Just as it is affected by each, they are affected by it. What would happen to the moon without the earth nearby? What would happen to the tides without the moon?

I will make three points. First, capitalism and the ultimate values affect and are affected by the academy. Second, cycles of social consciousness affect the direction of the academy, but they should not dictate it; and finally, strict adherence to its values priorities should enable the academy to serve to, through, and beyond the millennium.

Relationships with Capitalist Values

Capitalist values can be found everywhere in the American academy. Few should be surprised about that. Capitalism is the blessing and sometimes the curse of the nation. The quest for economic advantage has brought most people to our shores and many into higher education.

Institutions, including the academy, are capital-dependent. And the practitioners of the trade of higher education are similarly affected by the material, narcissistic, and conformist values of capitalism. The only problems occur when the impact becomes excessive, that is, when the values of scholarship and democracy are altered permanently by this challenge.

Scholarship supports the values of capitalism when truth is viewed as merely the discovery of facts, freedom as independence from others, and equality as conformity. Money becomes just another quantity for objective study—calibrated barter that can be assessed through the microscopes of science.

The democratic values of the academy can support capitalism too, but they draw it toward the bourgeois virtues. Community, justice, equality, and individuation acknowledge tangible men, women, and institutions as they are—but also as they would be.

Bourgeois business succeeds when it is smart and acknowledges long-term social principles. Mom's restaurant, offering home cooking and service with a smile, does not generate an image of crass capitalism, even if Mom does not live in the neighborhood. Such a business is founded on the principles of reciprocal interaction. It prospers when the owners provide a good product over time. Bourgeois virtue can be attained and maintained when a scholarly and democratic institution helps explore, define, and improve the benefits of mutual enterprise.

Relationships with the Ultimate Values

The scholarship values have been treated as middle-sized values throughout this book, to distinguish them from ultimate values such as beauty and spirituality. However, connections with the ultimate values cannot be snipped off or ignored. Eventually, the middle-sized truths of the academy must confront their relationship to Truth with a capital "T." The history of higher education has involved a human struggle to find lasting and unified truths as well as an acknowledgment of the difficulty in finding such truths through any methods of observation. Transcendent aesthetics and spirituality refract the essence of truth and the nature of human living. Aesthetics lies close to the scholarship interests of the academy because it integrates reason with emotion. Spirituality offers heart and faith to the scholarship values of the academy.

The scholarship values challenge false presentations of truth. Freedom, initial equality, and facts treated fairly disrupt convenient serenity and smug certainty. They prevent tyrants from imprisoning and biasing truth. And each day, the discoveries of modern physics and biology relate new facts to eternal mysteries. The theory of relativity is one absolute that is understood in many different ways.

The ultimate values of aesthetics and spirituality confirm the line and texture of humanity and, therefore, most of the democratic values of the academy. They are not outside the person as self, and through self with others. Not everyone can be an art collector, nor should everyone have that capitalistic ambition, but everyone should be art as well as spirit: emotional, contextual, and experiential. Human dignity is a primary interest of spirituality and aesthetics, and the academy adds human growing to it. One person growing helps all others. Together, the ultimate values and the academy fulfill the values of individuation and community.

Preferences for Challenger Values

It would be unreasonable to assume that any faculty have an innate bias toward particular challenger values. Despite any leanings they might have toward democratic or scholarship values, teaching faculty are. as likely to be interested in high consulting fees as researchers are. Church-related institutions include entrepreneurs as well as ministers. However, the proportionate interest in capitalism or the absolutes in any institution might be a function of the number of faculty, the curriculum, and the history of that institution. Smaller places are personalized by their inhabitants; in larger places people have to grasp for quantities of meaning.

In 1981, Donald Walker described the sacred and secular orientations of faculty and administrators to institutional governance. Some faculty interpret any administrator as a capitalist-in-hiding. In some cases, this perception is accurate, but the democratic values of the academy temper the capitalist tendencies of any such individuals. Nonprofit institutions do not usually seek nor succor isolated, narcissistic entrepreneurs. Conformity might be another matter, however, given the need of administrators to maintain a consistent identity within their institutions and for their institutions—so long as the budget remains balanced.

Cycles of Challenge and Change

In 1980, Arthur Levine popularized a theory that American higher education goes through cycles of individual and community ascendancy that are related to war. For example, periods of hot or cold war are times of ideological bigness. Individual identities are lost in group associations. Identities transfer from individual to local and national entities. John Jones becomes a GI. He dies and becomes a statistic in a body count. Statistics show the collective military strength of a nation, but they also dull the nation's awareness of the bloody realities of war (Hoopes, 1969). After the war, John Jones, Jr., emancipates himself from the group. He looks for personal instead of collective gains. He becomes an entrepreneur so that he can take care of personal business first. His dad might have died for his country, but Junior will live for himself.

Community ascendancy brings out the values of togetherness, justice, and growth in the academy. It is a time for teaching; research efforts are directed toward saving the world from itself. "We shall overcome" because education is necessary to save society. If the call for community is heard just before a war, as it was in the "new frontier" days of the early 1960s, then it brings with it concerns about equal rights and individuation. If it occurs during the war, then spirituality might become a bond, because God and country must be served by education. General education becomes citizenship education, binding individuals to the spirit of the nation.

After the war is over, the academy makes individuals stronger. "Peace and prosperity" was Eisenhower's campaign promise after the Korean War. Citizens could focus on individual advancement. Beaver Cleaver was going to beat Eddie Haskell at selling cars, but first he had to get into college. Then as now, a college education promised to put many more dollars in Beaver's wallet.

Max Lerner (1976) agreed that value systems are affected by any changes in a civilization and that values seem to appear in cycles. "The sixties were a little like the thirties in their values, the seventies are a little like the forties, but the cyclical swing doesn't return to its starting point, like the Oriental image of the serpent with its tail in its mouth. It returns, but from a different angle, at a different level. Moreover, a cultural organism like an individual one, constantly seeks equilibrium, even among its continuing storms" (p. 124). The circle might be unbroken, but its shape is certainly bent. World War II might have been a triumph of American technology and political bigness, but the Vietnam War revealed some weaknesses in both.

However, Lerner also wrote that values do not seem to change as radically as the rest of society. For example, Dan Quayle and Murphy Brown might have disagreed about the nature of the family but not about its importance. Values imply standards that resist the pressures of time and place. The value of family has endured profound changes in American attitudes toward sexuality, religion, and politics. So, then, the cycles or waves of change might seem more dramatic than they really are.

Real changes in values can never be perceived fully and accurately at any single point in time or within any particular context. There is the ever-present danger of presentism, that false reading of historical data through modern spectacles (Wilson, 1992). Presentism affects any reading of stability or change. It cannot be eliminated in any perspective, retrospective, or prospective of the academy, but its dangers can at least be acknowledged.

The academy rolls with the values of the time, now enmeshed in the stresses and strains of society, next standing aloof from it as an independent critic. Sometimes seeking new knowledge to triumph over an external enemy, the academy is next developing computers to win chess matches. Once teaching people how to ward off the Red menace, it is now teaching them about individual retirement accounts. When the community is most important, its values and priorities appear different than when the individual is.

The academy must fulfill its timeless obligations of scholarly and democratic service, and how that happens is affected by the weather outside. It helps to look through the window at the prevailing ethos. However, the actions of the academy do not rest entirely on what is happening outside it. In a time of individualism, the academy must remember its democratic teaching values and temper capitalistic ones. It must be a force of community in a society that does not seem to care about community at the time. In a time of community, the academy must maintain its scholarship purposes and confront easy absolutes. Truth tempers any mass movement. The solitary, truth-seeking scholar becomes a guide for the nation. In neither of these cases does the academy stress the popular. An anonymous source says that truth is something that is stranger than fiction, but never as popular. The academy must simply put first values first. In these two instances, however, the priority of some values does not exclude any values. The scholarship and democratic values still need to work together for the betterment of the academy and its nation.

This approach seems better than a simplistic synthesis of values. A too-certain synthesis of scholarship and democratic values should be a road less taken. By using the different values of the academy appropriately at different times, the academy provides a counterpoint to excessive capitalism and absolutism. It does not serve the nation by replicating other institutions or by having too lofty an opinion of itself.

Conclusion

A few years ago, Jaime Escalante spoke at the national conference of the American Association of Higher Education. He told the story of a student who was copying somebody else's answers on his tests. Escalante challenged the pupil about his cheating, and the next day the student's mother confronted Mr. Escalante, protesting that her son was innocent until proven guilty. "This is a free nation. How dare you talk about my son that way?" Mr. Escalante calmly said, "Let me show you something." He pulled out both of the students' papers. "Do you see this answer that the first student put on his paper? Pretty good. Your son's answer, identical. See this second one? It's excellent. And your son's, perfect. Now let me show you the third question. See here, the first student has put down, "I don't know." And here's your son's answer, "Me either."

As the nation approaches the millennium, more and more people will be asked to talk about the future of American higher education. None of them knows what will happen before the year 2001, much less afterward. Me either.

Most predictions will be wrong anyway. In 1979, it was predicted that higher education would lose 10 percent of its students and 25 percent of its small colleges during the 1980s, yet higher education gained 1.2 million students, and 60 percent of America's private colleges increased in size during that decade. The facts of higher education turned out differently than expected.

The uncertainty of facts is not just a millennial, centennial, annual, or even daily problem for the trustees, administrators, and faculty of any American college or university. Every moment, these people and their institutions face new situations that challenge established values with incomplete information.

The final part of this book deals with the manner and method of the responses to those challenges. It outlines the need for leaders—institutions and people—to clarify their values, to identify the values rumblings within any situation, and to express their values with value—with integrity.

Part Three

Advancing the Values We Prize

Thus far, this book has concentrated on the choosing and prizing of certain values. The final step of the valuing process is acting on them.

The time for action is at hand. This part discusses transmitting the values of the academy—transmitting them so that they are more solid and secure, more widely accessible, and more generously shared than we have received them.

Chapter Fourteen

Building an Identity Based on Values

Who are you? The first question posed in this book is asked again many pages later, but this time it is rephrased: *What* is your institution? What is the answer in one or two words, and what values lurk behind the answer? If the answer is "large," then the values might well be freedom, equality, and perhaps capitalism. They might also be individuation, community, and spirituality, although many pundits would be surprised by that declaration. Whatever the values, they would reveal the inner identity of the institution, that sense of self that makes it cohere and leads it into the future.

In Erik Erikson's (1968) scheme of human development, most adolescents are supposed to be creating the sexual, career, and ideological core of imminent adulthood. Later, they can find a life partner, a career, or children to make them productive; and then comes the wisdom of old age. It is a beautiful scheme, but many psychologists (and most middle-aged people) have noticed that this process of identity development does not stop with adolescence; it continues throughout the life span. The adolescent identity crisis has been joined by the mid-life crisis and, perhaps as soon as enough baby boomers reach retirement age, the old-codgers crisis.

As people grow older, they notice differences between the sense of self that they created in youth and the one they have or would prize now. Their old self-image differs from their present one, their old hopes from their current self-ideal. The baseball glove has sat in the closet ever since his shoulder gave out; he will never make the pros. Her beloved baby has gone off to college; she is not needed at home. Some parts of themselves stay the same, but others need removal and replacement.

As I noted in Chapter Six, adults often enter higher education because of some identity crisis. And as several authors noted during the late 1960s, the academy is not immune to such a crisis either. Thus, it is clear that identity development is a continuing struggle for people and institutions. To succeed in the struggle, it is important for people and institutions to reach inside and pull out the deepest values that guide them and explore new or additional ways to express those values. Some people will write books about their attempts to reach a new self-ideal. These might be books such as *Walden* or perhaps *The Vision Thing: Ways to Improve the Strategic Planning of Colleges and Universities*. The thrust is the same: to develop ways to draw the self-image closer to the self-ideal of the person or institution.

So far in this book, I have tried to explore and explain some of the values that affect the reality and ideals of the academy and the people within it. In this chapter, I provide some suggestions to make the self-ideal of the academy more real.

Manifesting Values

I present the suggestions for manifesting each value in no particular order, and they are not all-inclusive. I hope they will stimulate some readers to think more about the particular values they prize the most, as well as the ones their institutions should prize the most. Institutions should have a ready answer when someone asks, "What is your institution?"

Service

• Strategic planning should be based on the service mission of the academy. Mission statements should emphasize service. Functions and roles should be related to service. The explication of the service mission should yield greater public support for institutions of higher education, as well as more effective functioning inside those institutions.

• Each faculty and administrative group needs to examine the extent to which its "professionalism" is motivated toward better service or greater status. Special recognition might limit the effectiveness of endeavors that are synergetic forces in the academy. Those endeavors should evaluate whether some forms of recognition will help or hurt their service to the institution as a dynamic, whole entity.

• Faculty and administrators need to differentiate their basic obligations for service from their extraordinary efforts. Routine service duties should not overwhelm efforts to provide problem-solving and innovative seva-service. Personal development plans and annual reports should include and note these different types of service activities.

• "Public service" might be attached to every department title. For example, a Department of Public Service Physics might support collective membership in the society of Physicists Against the Spread of Nuclear Arms. A standard Department of Physics might be more content if none of its faculty belonged to such an association.

• It is very difficult to measure long-term service instead of short-term services. As a result, faculty, staff, and institutional service has been measured by the quantity of activities instead of their eventual merit. This deters individuals and institutions from participating in some areas of social service. However, no institution is in a better position to measure social service than the academy, and it should devote resources to measuring its long-term impact on the commonweal.

• The mantle of "expert" limits academic participation in some social betterment activities. The academy should rely on its learning role instead, helping to gather resources, information, and personnel for the analysis and resolution of knotty social problems. If we do not have answers right now, we can still prove that we are good at finding them.

Truth

• Every graduate should experience all the forms of truth. Liberal education must include the deliberate development of reading, writing, and reckoning; the development of inquisitive observation; and analytical, integrating experience. In addition, every graduate should understand the interrelationships among the three forms of academic truth.

- Practicing the habits of scrupulousness, doubt, and tolerance is more convincing than any lecture on truth. These habits should be affirmed in every course that students take and modeled by every professor in the classroom, as well as the laboratory.
- Faculty as well as students need to develop their own skills of reading, writing, and reckoning. All should review the list of books that St. John's or a similar institution requires and read at least one of them soon. One hundred specialized dissertations might not equal one classic. The professor who complains, "I'm doing so much reading that I never have time to improve my mind," ought to read something different.
- Time is not a bad measure of truth, when time is supported by contemporary data. The classic ideas provide skeletons of truths on which current observations and opinions can be hung.
- Some social scientists dismiss the refined reasoning that empiricism demands, but just as a classic book can benefit all readers, so can a classic method of reasoning benefit all reckoners. Every faculty member should practice seeing how objective he or she can be in analyzing a professional issue before taking a stand about it. The way to truth is as important as the light.
- Students are pragmatists. Their experiences in classes can be a starting point rather than the concluding point of their search for truth. Professors can work backward from experience to research and reading. They can begin with the actor, then move to the action, and finally to the idea.

Freedom

- The rights and responsibilities of faculty need to be clarified regarding service activities that involve scholarship outside the academy, for example, whether there are limits to social advocacy and political activities, when faculty serve nonprofit associations.
- American faculty should remind themselves of the blessings inherent in the practice of their trade in a free nation. Other faculty have died for the freedom to voice their intelligence.
- Scientists, artists, and social scientists must act as application scholars, maintaining the virtues of scrupulousness, doubt, and tolerance whether they are acting as citizens or academicians in regard to social issues.

• Society questions most the alliances between academic, political, and commercial agencies. Therefore, institutional policies, administrators, and faculty must make these alliances as few and as uneasy as possible. Absolute clarity is needed at all times in answering the question, Who owns what knowledge?

• Few faculty understand the perils faced by ethical administrators who must appease political and economic agencies while preserving the fundamental mission of the institution. Such administrators have no tenure to rely on; they speak out at their own risk, and they deserve support whenever they do.

• The educational function of the academy should place student freedoms at the front and not the rear of the discussion of academic freedom. If laws cannot protect students from crudeness, then at least students should be taught their rights and given the skills to challenge barbarians wherever they find them.

Equality

• The community college is America's bellwether of access and success. It needs to be studied systematically. For example, some states are beginning to ask whether they should restrict the provision of remedial education to community colleges instead of supporting those courses in public four-year institutions. Higher education should encourage, embrace, and expand formal examinations of such topics before they result in premature political action.

• The issues of affirmative action affect cultural, economic, and political equality. They are not restricted to academic opportunity. The study of affirmative action also needs to be encouraged, embraced, and expanded.

• Recommendations in the justice and freedom chapters apply to the value of equality. Justice determines the rights of the collective or the individual. Fairer opportunities for all are necessary for individuals to be free. In addition, students need to learn how to use opportunities for the advancement of all.

• Traditional faculty authority has dwindled as budgets have been cut and institutions have grown more hierarchical or anarchical. Their collegial authority remains strong, and they remain the central authority in educating students about equality.

• Many faculty and administrators can provide personal testimonials to equal opportunity, since they have used the meritocratic system to rise from socioeconomic disadvantage. Many are first-generation college students. They are like the successful orderly in *I Never Promised You a Rose Garden* (Greenberg, 1964), who helped the patients because he understood that he was not very different from them. Their stories must be used widely and well.

Individuation

• Professors and administrators must never give up on their own development, since their most important teaching comes through modeling the developing life.

• The academy must help students to be alone. This is easy on the residential campus, but it is just as necessary for commuters. If physical isolation is impossible, then symbolic isolation can be attained when reflective journals, autobiographies, and other assignments require students to acquire, absorb, and integrate information that builds their singularity.

• The involving campus builds individuation and community. The most important involvements are between faculty and students outside the classroom. This is nearly impossible in commuter campuses, where the students with greatest need encounter part-time faculty who teach at several different campuses each day in order to assemble full-time employment. These students need at least one assigned mentor who will be available to them at lunch, dinner, and other times and places outside the usual.

• Student affairs administrators see students when they are most vulnerable. They have counseling skills and reasons for relating to students that are not always within the repertoire of faculty. Teams of student affairs and faculty personnel have been effective in co-teaching orientation courses, and they might be sustained as contact units throughout the two-, four-, or six-year experience of students on campus.

• Colleges might consider stimulating a search for the most unforgettable characters on campus. Years ago, *Reader's Digest* published essays about such individuals. The essays were heartwarming testimonials that boosted the creative possibilities of the self. They would also support those men and women on any campus who teach themselves to students, as well as their subject matter.

Justice

• Strategic planning procedures might be applied to the development of substantive justice on campus. A substantive justice mission statement could be developed, as well as clear procedures that make the mission attainable.

• The parallel with strategic planning provides forewarning. Too often, institutions get so mired in abstractions or details that the strategic planning process fails. This might be even easier in substantive justice planning, but it must not happen.

• The furor about affirmative action programs is primarily about finances, but affirmative practices often demand more time than money. Individuals who are committed to affirmation can redistribute their time in order to make extra telephone calls to candidates, to spend more time tutoring students who need assistance, and to encourage fair treatment in all matters that concern students inside and outside the classroom.

• Grading systems should be altered so that students can assess their progress as well as their levels of attainment. In the absence of such a formal system, individual faculty should be sure that students know how their talent is developing. "A" students should know when a professor thinks they are coasting, and "F" students should know when they are moving forward.

• Approximately 85 percent of all instruction is offered through lectures, but justice requires a conversation rather than a monologue. All sides should be presented fairly and then decisions encouraged about subject matter. Critical thinking is as essential to justice as it is to truth.

Community

• Cohort executive programs establish communities for students who would otherwise be isolated commuters. Small liberal arts colleges might have the most success in offering these programs, since they emulate the personal character, if not the curricula, of these institutions. Cohort graduate programs have been successful in large universities as well. Cohorts are especially important at the crisis times of higher education, for example, upon entry, when declaring a major, or during the writing of a dissertation.

• Living-learning centers, academic houses, and other programs have been successful in building a sense of residential community, but they need to be expanded to meet the needs of commuter populations. The notion of territoriality needs to be enhanced. Commuter students need to "own" designated areas of campuses. These can be study rooms in libraries or unused rooms in residence halls, where commuters can leave their belongings and build their belongingness.

• The integrative purpose of liberal learning has not been emphasized during the debate about the Western and multicultural canons. Integrative purposes should be more important than the intellectual jihad that separates components of the curriculum. And experiences need to integrate insight with action, for example, the sense of vocation that is literally a calling with the efforts that are often known as work.

• In one hour, the president can initiate a twenty-four-hour conversation among all parties in an academy. Presidents might set aside a time for brown bag lunches once a week or once a month. Students can be selected at random for the lunches; so might faculty. Or else the president might just take a seat by the nearest campus monument and see what the people walking by have to say.

• The celebrative aspect of community is often ignored. Every campus has its special monuments and rites. Even though public historically black colleges have been integrated since 1954, the monuments of their original heroes need to be polished. Every student needs to know the identity of the people whose names are on the buildings. Celebration does not just build a sense of belonging. It builds pride.

Capitalism

• In Chapter Two, I confirmed that altruistic service is difficult for anyone to maintain for a long time and that no one should disregard good service that yields personal rewards. If they are helped to focus on the concrete, personal gains of egoistic altruism, more faculty and administrators will be willing to build the moral spirit and the sense of community on their campuses. Even if they do not intend to do fully the right thing, they will do more things right.

- Many students do not have sufficient motivation to achieve, because they cannot see the benefits to themselves of their own enterprise. Nor are they connected to enterprise teams, that is, success teams that mutually develop skills. The model of junior achievers could be applied to the college campus, especially with first-generation students who lack support for their success from people off-campus.
- Enterprise teams are useful for other groups, too. Team play used to be discussed in every book on women's management. Men have experienced team sports and women have not; when they play sports, women value teamwork more than standing out as stars. One-on-one competitions against a lecturer must be supplemented with more team play in classes, and outside.
- Quality improvement approaches have combined consumerism with strategic planning. For a change, the student is placed first instead of last in these approaches. The priority is appropriate educationally and politically, since the reform of higher education has focused on teaching students, and the reform of business has focused on consumer service. If the primary product of higher education is student learning, then the quality approach must prove more eternal than ephemeral. If the student is a consumer instead of a product, then, as Chris de Winter Hebron (1993) argues, colleges need to adopt a Students' Rights Charter to help define the duties, services, and ownerships directed at their clients.

Spirituality

- The need for unity remains strong, even though the search for truth opposes easy unity unprobed by intellect. It is not necessary to dismiss the need for unity while probing its boundaries.
- The first principles of the academy must be articulated with passion and certainty. While academic truth rests more comfortably in the middle realm of values, it does not end there. Whether or not the end of truth stretches to God or just into space is unimportant, the passion of seeking it, the values involved in finding it, and the service of truth must be articulated as ultimate principles of the academy.
- Truth must be fulfilled through wise, loving action. Spirituality seeks good deeds performed by full individuals. Some of the

suggestions about service are related to spirituality, since selfless service is a link between spirit and the academy.

• "Hate the sin but not the sinner" is an edict of faith. In this case, it might be interpreted as hating the false separation of intellect from love and good deeds. Unthinking zealots must be opposed, but they can be opposed with reason and passion. Intellect might exist without referents, but it is not separate from any other human conditions.

• The spiritual values of unity and universal love remind the academy that intellectual snobbery is not only impolite—it is wrong. Everyone deserves basic love, and everyone can share in the love of learning that the academy represents. Individual communities of mutual empowerment may exclude whom they wish, but the love of universal learning can be cherished by all.

Aesthetics

• Aesthetics is tied to liberal education and, thus, to the classical purposes of higher education; the skillful administrator and professor will make this connection within the division, with academicians and with cabinet officers, when explaining the importance of aesthetic activities.

• Some have always had aesthetics management responsibilities. Through art exhibits, clean residence halls, and the college viewbook, administrators maintain and promote the beauty of the campus. This affects enrollment management, campus relations, and student development. The importance of this aesthetics management role should be understood and emphasized.

• The psychological development of students requires the development of aesthetic sensibilities. Faculty and student affairs professionals should coordinate their efforts in this area of student development.

• The assessment movement has failed to use aesthetics to assess demographics, facilities, and programs. For example, residential life patterns could be analyzed according to the density, repleteness, and symbolization of students in the halls. A "portrait" of people, programs, and facilities could be drawn, then room and hall assignments modified to improve the residential life system and, ultimately, the development of a holistic campus environment.

• Perceiving students as art improves teaching and advising. Aesthetics reminds world-weary faculty of the uniqueness of these individuals, and it promotes the use of techniques like metaphorical analysis in the counseling relationship.

• Aesthetics provides a unique way to improve cultural diversity on campus, both through explicit activities and through aesthetic analysis. Aesthetics belongs to no single cultural group, sex, or academic cohort. It can be used to enhance, justify, and gain acceptance for cultural diversity efforts in classrooms, student centers, and residence halls.

• Aesthetics makes up the "art" of good administration, which Frank Borelli (1984) describes as the blending of technical skills with vision. Aesthetics justifies the passion and intuition that are part of administration. It organizes emotion with intellect. While this aspect of aesthetics is not tangible, it is absolutely necessary for good practice. Aesthetics teaches administrators how to show that they care.

Conclusion

One maxim of behavioral psychotherapy is that action, not insight, is ultimately curative. And one aspect of values is that they are guides to action. They appeal to the doer as much as to the dreamer. Values are not wordy statements. They are not even mission statements. They are declared in one or two words, and then they must be used. Players do not have to hear a lecture beforehand and then, groggy from the words, stumble toward the playing field.

In ideal schemes, action comes after values have been declared, but the process is rarely that straightforward. In the next chapter, I focus on ways in which values can be used with integrity, during times of conflict instead of calm. The call is out for leadership: values will become clear before, during, and after the game has been won.

Chapter Fifteen

Using Values with Integrity

The final chapter of this book is dedicated to integrity, that expression of self that draws honorable action from insight. Since no values can be seen, tasted, or felt, all must be inferred from attitudes, actions, and words. Those words, actions, and attitudes might as well have integrity about them. They should be honorable.

Saying the word "integrity" is not the same as living it. Stephen Carter (1996), the author of a book on the subject, knows this. Carter believes that integrity requires more than discerning what is right and what is wrong. It means acting on what has been discerned, even at personal cost, and saying openly that one is trying to do what is right. A person might be entirely honest without engaging in the hard work that integrity requires.

Carter also believes that integrity is most honorable when a person risks self-interest for the sake of others, but he recognizes that integrity and self-interest can coincide. This book is based on the same reality: purely selfless service is most moral, but no one should turn down an opportunity to help others, even if he or she gains from the process. Integrity offers the same reward.

Integrity fulfills the honor inherent in values. For example, Walter Muelder (1978) defines integrity in higher education as devotion to the wholeness of the individual and to truth; it is freedom expressed responsibly. Drawn from social and ultimate values, the academy with integrity helps people to function effectively as community members instead of capitalists. Thus, Muelder's opinions summarize much of the book so far, invoking essential values of individuation, truth, freedom, community, and service. How to go about achieving this integrity becomes the next question to be addressed.

That process—the quest for integrity—is the topic of this chapter. The quest is akin to the hero's adventure, which Joseph Campbell describes with great passion and insight. Therefore, many of the points of this chapter follow the model that Campbell initiated in his 1949 work, *The Hero with a Thousand Faces*. First, however, I discuss discernment—what Carter considered to be the hardest work of integrity. This involves rational planning before the leader has any sense of the values adventure ahead. Second, I discuss values conflicts, because they are the emotional scourge of models of rational planning. Third, I describe the elements of the leader's adventure and follow those in sequence from preparation, through confrontation, to reflection, and finally, to lasting meaning. The term *leader* has the potential to be attached to many people and institutions, just as Campbell made the role of hero accessible to one and all. However, the title must be earned.

Discernment

Every leader, institution, or individual is familiar with rational planning models. Their titles change, but their basic elements remain the same. Whether they are called Big Mac or Big Boy or CQI or outcomes assessment, they are essentially the same burgers and buns. Rational planning models set priorities before actions are needed. Most of them include four stages, beginning with awareness, then decision making, then action components, and ending with an evaluative process that renews awareness. They are process models, with no results guaranteed, and sometimes the process is as important as the product, because the involvement of many people in the awareness stage builds ownership and commitment to the choices and actions that ensue.

Variations on the theme of awareness sell most books. This stage is the easiest to write about because the pressures of decision making and action are least immediate. Theory can be added to the awareness stage; planners tap generalizations for insight. Or the models can involve different people in this stage. Still other models can acknowledge preliminary judgments in the first component of planning, for example, the values clarification model of Louis Raths, Merrill Harmin, and Sidney Simon (1966) includes an evaluation of what is prized before choices are made and actions are performed. E*valuation* comes before as well as after the process.

It is important to expand the discernment or awareness stage as much as possible in order for acts of integrity to arise from the planning process. The perception of value *before* might be as important as value *added,* because it declares what is important to the people who will take part in the leadership quest, before the quest begins.

Valuing adds the imperative adjectives and verbs that the organization or individual has collected and must now dust off. Value words add intensity to the cause, and that intensity will be necessary during the tests of leadership. Valuing helps make decisions conscientious instead of merely conscious. It increases the likelihood that actions will be initiated and sustained, and it increases the likelihood of reflection after the battle is done.

Valuing also accents the uniqueness of the planning context. Different hues are apprehended and applied in different ways to different situations. Textbook models do not provide this color if they do not contain values approaches. An example of the difference comes to mind. A few years ago, a meeting was held in a department of educational administration about the future of the leadership course in higher education. One professor, a former principal, wanted to eliminate that course and replace it with a generic leadership course that he intended to teach. Another, the recently retired president of the university where the course was being taught, objected to the plan. He said that the context and values of higher education prevented generic instruction from being fully effective. To this, the other person responded, "You don't have enough experience in this field to make that statement!"

The same illogic is applied by the authors of leadership books that are based on profit-making enterprise, when those authors do not understand the values-in-context of nonprofit agencies, education in general, and higher education in particular. Unless the specific traditions of value are explored within the contexts of leadership, integrity will not be revealed through their designs.

Values Conflict and Leadership

Conflict is inherent in any planning situation. Otherwise, there is no need to plan. Applications are down, the college of business disagrees with arts and sciences, alumni dislike changes at their university, and the football team is not winning. Some of these conflicts are clearly related to values. Alexander Astin (1989) notes that institutions have both explicit and implicit values. The mission statement, catalogue, charter, and public records convey the explicit values, but the values that drive the institution underlie these words. They are found in funding policies, decisions about hiring, curriculum and teaching priorities, and facility priorities. Some inconsistencies are inevitable between the explicit and implicit values. However, Astin thinks that the most demoralizing situations in the academy occur when an institution's actions do not reflect its values as they are expressed by its president or its publications.

Leaders with integrity understand and reduce the conflicts. They identify and use the right values when they act. This concept is confirmed by examining a device that is used by many authors of leadership books—making distinctions between competent and excellent leadership. An example is illustrated by Warren Bennis's phrase, "Leaders do the right thing; managers do things right." Integrity is the right thing done. Peter Vaill (1991) has written that leaders articulate values, and they teach people how to embrace and use values. Managers discover values conflicts and work out ways to solve the conflicts. James McGregor Burns (1978) has distinguished transformative from transactional leaders. Transformative leadership is value-centered behavior that helps both leaders and followers reach the highest levels of motivation, morality, and satisfaction. Transactional leadership deals with the exchange of valued goods or ideas.

The Leader's Adventure

Stephen Carter writes that "integrity is a journey" (Wicker, 1996). Integrity is more a verb than a noun; like all true values, it is dynamic instead of fixed. Values are made real through good works. The context and need for such works vary, but the sequence of valuing might not. Leaders who increase awareness now are better prepared to decide and act in any situation that might arise later. They—people, departments, organizations—have prepared themselves for an adventure ahead.

Joseph Campbell (1949, 1988, 1989) has written about the hero's adventure as expressed in mythology. The hero goes through a sequence of events that is everywhere the same—in economics, art, or higher education. The person or organization senses its own potential but does not know how to achieve it. A sense of danger arises. Huge problems emerge that are opportunities disguised. The leader is challenged and must respond. If he or she—or the institution—does not respond, the adventure is over, but if the response succeeds, a new consciousness is gained, a consciousness that the leader uses to educate others. The last phase is as active and important as the first, at least in Western mythology. While an Indian yogi might never return from a journey into personal enlightenment, one with a will to serve others must never escape the world. The adventure must end with the wisdom and the power to serve others. This person, group, or institution does not live only for itself, because leading is more than mere celebrity. It acts to redeem society.

The Campbell sequence was put into a workbook by Lorna Catford and Michael Ray (1991) called *The Path of the Everyday Hero*. The authors identify the stages of the hero's adventure as innocence, the call to adventure, initiation, allies, breakthrough, and celebration. They relate each of these stages to the creative experiences of preparation, frustration, incubation, strategizing, illumination, and verification. Catford and Ray emphasize the creativity of heroism; here I am calling it *leadership*. The nouns that they apply to the stages do not matter, but the act of leading does. In this chapter, I will describe the stages as apprehension, preparation, initiation, and education.

Apprehension

The institution or person is doing well. The sewers do not overflow, and the bills are paid. The bureaucracy is functioning, and relationships seem fine, too, even in a large institution. Faculty, students, and board members are not acting up. However, this contentment might be apathy shrouded in normalcy and any progress within the institution, just middle-aged survival. A friend comes up to the president and says that the only difference between a rut and a grave are the dimensions. Shallow laughter covers the deep remark.

Joseph Campbell said that work begins when you do not like what you are doing. It applies to people and places. The pressures to conform are ever-present, and what looks like progress is practiced coasting. The researcher studies the specializations of specialized phenomena. The professor offers up yet another semi-annual lecture. The counselor shares his personal experiences with a student, just one more time. The president picks up a copy of the new five-year vision plan, which looks very much like the last mission plan, or perhaps that was the strategic plan that was developed in 1985.

The values in these situations are submerged within the iterations of daily life. They are not made plain enough. Leaders react to external stimuli, but a profound sense of self drives few. However, something is starting to stir inside those who prize integrity. The twitchings might start in familiar places, such as authorities that are trusted, personal logic, sense experiences, emotions, intuition, or scientific techniques (Lewis, 1990), but their sources are not as important as the recognition of the symptoms at this time, and then what they stimulate leaders to do.

Leaders, whether people or places, are not complacent. They seek to serve. They pay attention to values twitchings. Some will begin to ponder their future and whether they still have the knightly virtues that charmed Campbell—loyalty, temperance, and courage—although this pondering will be subconscious at first, and then conscious but silent to themselves. To what degree are they loyal to their ideals or their daily work? Can they still be brave? Their desire to do and be more chafes against their maintenance of the status quo. Eventually, the specialist realizes that he still has an inkling of a great idea; the professor a new lecture; the finance officer a way to truly right-size the organization: the manager feels the twinkling of the leader within.

Preparation

Preparation begins when the leader clarifies what is right—or wrong. Thirty years ago, Raths, Harmin, and Simon (1966) popularized the term and the process of "values clarification," a rational process for examining one's heartfelt guides. However, these authors did not advocate any rights, wrongs, or priorities for persons, much less institutions. Their process was personal and contextual, and this upset many who wanted a list of values preclarified, a list that supported their current beliefs without making them think about what they believed.

This maintenance strategy works for most people when the challenges of internal and external life do not demand too much, and the rut does not seem too deep. However, the leader who is in dis-ease wants more. That leader will use the time to examine values. The person or institution will start gathering evidence, to understand at least the intensity and extent of the discomfort.

Clarification

Since so much has been written about values clarification on a personal level, this discussion will use similar principles and examples from the institutional perspective. The values audit has been used to examine institutional purposes and perspectives. It has been promoted during the awareness stage of strategic planning, the time of preparation before the good fight.

In *Managing as a Performing Art,* Peter Vaill (1991) balances the benefits of values-driven enterprises against the detriments of values-muddled ones, of integrity against anguish. He offers ten principles for clarifying organizational values. First, values must be uncovered within the content of communication, because values are inferred from other indicators. Second, the values must be stated and restated evenhandedly. Third, the relativity of most values must be overcome; all deserve consideration. Fourth, nobody must lose in the process. Values clarification helps an institution in proportion to the number of people who believe that their values are involved. Fifth, Vaill reminds his readers that values are displayed in actions. What we do (and do not do) reveals our values. Sixth, helpful mechanisms can ease the process. Seventh, the core values of people are extremely important. These values reflect a person's sense of self, linking again leadership of the institution with the individual. The eighth principle is to not suppress actions, because these are also symbolic expressions of a person's values. Ninth, the closer the process is to the work of the organization, the more that organizational survival and effectiveness will support the process. Vaill's last point is a reminder that values are nonlogical. "I do not mean *illogical* which implies that values are antirational. . . . *Nonlogical* means that, at the core, the meaning to a person of a particular value is not decided by logic and reason" (p. 58).

Institutional values audits manifest these principles. These audits build awareness in strategic planning. They involve people because of their ethical and emotional essence. They provide a forum for shared reflection by all the members of the community of mutual empowerment. In addition, they reveal the existence of and relationships among expressed and actual values. They point out consensus and conflict, and they provide a different way of analyzing accomplishments and problems (Smith, 1985).

Many of the first values audits were conducted in religiously affiliated institutions. The colleges of character know that they have values, know what those values are, and know that these values must be revealed through institutional actions. Their problems are not with relativistic values as much as with the active relating of absolute ones.

In 1985, the Society for Values in Higher Education conducted a study about values and decision making in higher education (Smith and Reynolds, 1990). This study involved eight diverse colleges and universities and was intended to "create portraits of the [campus] cultures as systems of values, complete with the values tensions that were the root of disagreements in various decision-making areas" (p. 25). A later, 1989 study sought to identify the core values in six Catholic colleges and universities and to determine how they were communicated, and whether the identified values were shared, by whom, and to what degree (Murphy, 1990). In 1991, the Council of Independent Colleges sponsored the National Institute on Values and Education: Developing Personal and Public Ethics. Institutional teams completed a mission analysis, values audit, and tentative values plan. During the institute, the teams also reviewed and critiqued the values plans of the other institutions.

Public institutions seem to be joining the process. For example, the Kellogg Founda ion has established a Commission on the Future of State and Land Grant Universities. Gordon Gee (1996), chairman of the Commission and president of Ohio State University, wrote that it has identified five key areas to meet a straightforward goal—to help these institutions set a new standard for excellence. The five key areas are values areas: access, engagement (meaning productive contact with the community), a learning society, student experience (making students a higher priority), and faculty-campus culture (balancing research and teaching). Gee related these institutional values to a higher purpose: "The Kellogg

Commission is the best opportunity we have to frame the debate about the future of public higher education in America—in many ways, the debate about the future of America itself" (p. 9a).

Temptation

The leader's apprehension increases. The twitching becomes a severe tic. The values audit might establish long-term priorities, but it bares as well those conflicts and incompletenesses that increase the emotional dis-ease of troubled institutions. Leaders in these places have begun their adventure already. In other places, leaders encounter more subtle omens. Perhaps temptations will arise. Campbell writes that the temptations of Jesus were universally valid. The first was economic, being able to survive. The second was political, coping with the extent of power that a person would have. The last was spiritual, overcoming the aura of exceptional morality. Campbell also talked about the temptations of Buddha. The first was desire for something greater. The second was fear of death, and the third was duty—concrete or spiritual. These temptations can seduce the well-being and service of every place and person, including academies with their professors and presidents.

The call to adventure grows louder. Something disrupts the familiar: perhaps a student is murdered; a sports team is put on probation; or the endowment collapses. The call must be ignored or answered now. The unprepared person ignores the call, according to Campbell, "because it's safe and secure, then life dries up. And then he comes to that condition in late middle age: he's gotten to the top of the ladder, and found it's against the wrong wall" (Campbell, 1989, p. 24). The leader prepared will decide, act, and return with knowledge that serves.

Initiation

On June 6, 1994, a *New York Times* editorial described the fiftieth anniversary of Operation Overlord—the D-Day invasion. The battle was won by a handful of eighteen- to twenty-year-old soldiers and sailors whose comrades died by scores. "What lifted and moved them went beyond military science, courage, and fear into the realm of the intangible. Overlord could not have succeeded without the mortar of trust and shared values" (p. A10).

The initiation stage includes three components. First, the leader accepts the need to lead. Second, allies might be discovered. Finally, the leader fulfills integrity with decisive acts.

Accepting the Challenge

The camel is straining from the load of straws. They might not seem dramatic individually, but they sum impressively. The last straw does not break the camel's back but only seems to; the accumulated weight of the straws does that job. Still, that last straw— professor, student, administrator, politician—must be dealt with before the camel gives out. Campbell says that this is when the leader must slay the first dragon, Thou Shalt, and its equally evil twin, Thou Shalt Not. The leader will respect the rules of society, legal procedure, and faculty contracts, but the leader will not be subdued by them, or by the apparent mass of the camel they ride on.

Allies

Preparation is the leader's greatest ally. The leader is partially ready for the adventure if he or she has begun the clarification process, and even more ready if he or she has done so thoroughly, directly, and in a leisurely way before the crisis ensues. The crisis demands action more than insight. Time is a luxury, so others cannot be called for extended counsel. The leader seems to be in the wilderness alone. However, a few other allies might provide assistance, even now.

Campbell says that other allies might emerge to help our leader, just in the nick of time. Strangers come to the leader just when he or she recognizes that personal change is necessary to continue the adventure with integrity. The strangers give the leader some sort of instrument to help with the adventure, something that includes psychological commitment and a psychological center. The commitment goes beyond intention to the merger of the hero with the event. The stranger helps the leader fulfill the creative process through focusing the values center inside himself or herself.

The ally is a teacher, a shaman older and wiser, who knows how to play the fool in the king's court when necessary. The shaman has not read the book about the adventure—he or she has experienced it. The fool may mock the court, because the king knows that he gains wisdom from someone who is beyond his control.

Many allies have experienced the values quest for integrity. Two of them are LeMoyne College in Syracuse and Alverno College in Wisconsin. LeMoyne was one of eight colleges that participated in the pilot study by the Society of Values in Higher Education. After its involvement in the study, LeMoyne created a values program that has three dimensions: an annual summer institute with a value-laden theme such as war and peace or economic justice that can be related to curriculum and instruction, an academic forum that seeks to integrate the summer theme throughout the year, and continuing research and evaluation. As a result of its own experiences, Alverno College has vowed to graduate students who are competent in eight abilities, among them valuing, communicating, analyzing, problem solving, interacting socially, taking responsibility for the global environment, demonstrating effective citizenship, and responding aesthetically.

An individual ally might also be available, a values shaman who has authored himself or herself through a quest for integrity. Who has surmounted crises of service, truth, freedom, equality, individuation, justice, and community? Who is willing to teach others how to internalize and then use such experiences? And who just wants to sell a personal story through lectures or books? Early identification and access to a true ally saves time later, when external consulting is not needed as much as internal transforming. Necessity must be distinguished from her handmaidens. Values actions are due.

Some of these allies might offer instruments to the leader, such as values decision-making models. Values decision-making models help the leader reflect-in-action, when values like theories are tested as they are being developed, during the adventure. Donald Schön (1987), an architect of reflective decision making, believes that a leader is a researcher in the context of practice, freed from established theory and techniques, and charged with the task of constructing a new theory to fit the unique situation that the adventure presents.

Formal models of values decision making differ from clarification models in two ways. They assess conflicts instead of possibilities, and they provide some information about how to resolve a conflict with integrity. For example, Richard Morrill (1981) writes about three components in the assessment stage of decision making: values analysis to study the values inherent to the situation; values consciousness to clarify the values in this particular situation; and values criticism, to discover the conflicts or contradictions within a personal or social system. The last stage often seems to occur first during the leader's adventure. Morrill calls the resolution stage "values pedagogy." Here, leaders develop and defend their own positions, deeply probe the justifications for their choices, confront standards and points of view that are in opposition to their own perspectives, and assume the role of someone with a contrasting point of view.

Another decision-making model has been advanced by Karen Kitchener (1984). In the first level of her model, the facts of the situation and the ordinary moral sense of the leader combine to form intuitive judgments and actions. These should be guided, refined, and evaluated through a critical-evaluative process that includes rules such as professional codes and laws, ethical principles or values, and ethical theory. Kitchener suggests using five values that she derived from medical ethics: beneficence, autonomy, nonmaleficence, justice, and fidelity.

These models are allies to the decision maker, but still, like all paper and pen diagrams, they suggest general procedures and sequences. No model guides actions about any particular context or crisis. Nor can the leader identify entirely with the experience of any individual or institutional ally.

Thus, the instruction from any ally is not instruction *per se*. As Walter Turnbull (1995), the founder of the Boys Choir of Harlem, says, "Integrity can't really be taught. What's most important is providing an environment in which . . . [one] can learn integrity, an environment where discipline is important, where honesty is important, where courage is important, where love is important. All those things" (p. 10). Campbell uses the story of Theseus and Ariadne to make the same point. Ariadne gives Theseus a ball of string to unwind as he goes through the labyrinth that surrounds him. She does not take him out. "That's all you need—an Ariadne thread." The ally's job is to give the leader the thread, to show the way to truth, not to show the truth itself. "All a teacher can do is suggest" (Campbell, 1988, p. 150).

Action

The situations differ, but in each of them the leader walks through the conflict into the future without looking back. A far less perilous parallel occurs when any student enters the library at the University of Rochester. On one side of the doors is a frieze that declares, "Here is the history of human ignorance, error, superstition, folly, war and waste recorded by human intelligence for the admonition of wiser ages still to come." On the other side of the doors is inscribed, "Here is the history of man's hunger for truth, goodness, and beauty, leading him slowly on through flesh to spirit, from bondage to freedom, from war to peace." The student walks through the doors bearing their own inscription, "The doors of the past open to those who seek to know what has been—the history of the stars, the earth, sunlight, life and man's long journey; the doors of the present open to those who seek to know what man can do—to master his fate by science, sustain his spirit by art, and guide his life by wisdom; [and] the doors of the future open to those who wonder what life may become—when men are free in body and soul, loving all beauty, serving in many ways one God."

Education

A child's fairy tale about heroes ends with the dragon slain and the hero living happily ever after. The real story differs. Heroes and leaders might triumph only over their own fears, lose their jobs, and continue to educate others—without glory but with honor. Integrity is not outside but inside first, where all values root. The adventure has enabled the leaders to identify, reconcile, and synthesize values. They are transformed—a process that began with the slaying of the first dragons, Thou Shalt and Thou Shalt Not. Campbell says that these leaders are people who have discerned the inevitable and got in front of it. They have sacrificed themselves for a people, a person, or an idea. Now they must return to the world and make their values known anew. That is difficult because their adventure into integrity will be judged by others who cannot understand the leaders' accomplishments or know how to continue them.

The leader empowers the community by returning to it, even when people within do not understand what has happened during the adventure. In addition, the leader finalizes the rational process by evaluating what has occurred. This person or institution must reflect-*on*-action and refurbish the awareness that initiated the process. The leader might have a half hour before a new adventure begins and perhaps not even that long. The leader's experience will be helpful next time.

Campbell finalizes his perspective of the leader-hero by summing two of his aspects. This leader is someone you can lean on and someone who represents an ideal. This leader can become an ally to others who pursue the integrity of valuing. In addition, the leader models integrity to others inside the community and outside it. Some will know that the leader's actions of value have followed discernments of values. The leader—person or institution—has created the value being of itself.

Conclusion

When John Coleman was president of Haverford, he took a sabbatical in order to work at various blue-collar jobs. His book about this adventure, *Blue Collar Journal* (1974), concluded with the tale of Zusia, the Hasidic rabbi who said, "When I shall face the celestial tribunal, I shall not be asked why I was not Abraham, Jacob, or Moses. I shall be asked why I was not Zusia."

Fulfilling the trust of values is first a personal adventure. It includes comprehension and composition as well as action. At eighty-two years of age, Joseph Campbell said that his life seemed almost as orderly as a composed novel. The little accidental meetings turned out to be main features in the plot, and what seemed to have been mistakes at the time turned out to be directive crises.

The comfort of composition is due those who pursue the valuing life in general and within the academy in particular. These leaders seek first to serve beyond themselves. Fundamental altruism underlies their actions, and it is supported by other values that fulfill the trust.

The academy cannot wait for others to recognize the need for its value in society; it cannot yield to simplistic capitalism or rely on self-righteous academic values for succor. The academy must lead with integrity in order to serve society, not to be saved by society. This is not just its legal requirement, it is its moral opportunity, and thus its essential obligation.

References

"Altruism Is in Style." *U.S. News and World Report,* 1994, pp. 25–33.

American Association of Colleges of Nursing (AACN). *Essentials of College and University Education for Nursing: A Working Document.* Washington, D.C.: American Association of Colleges of Nursing, 1986.

American Association of University Professors. "The 1915 Declaration of Principles." Reprinted in L. Joughlin (ed.), *Academic Freedom and Tenure.* Madison, Wis.: The University of Wisconsin Press, 1967. (Originally published 1915.)

American Association of University Professors. "Statement of Principles on Academic Freedom and Tenure." Reprinted in L. Goodchild and H. Wechsler (eds.), *The History of Higher Education.* Needham Heights, Mass.: Ginn Press, 1989. (Originally published 1940.)

American Council on Education. "The Student Personnel Point of View." Reprinted in G. Saddlemire and A. Rentz (eds.), *Student Affairs: A Profession's Heritage.* Media Publication, no. 40. Alexandria, Va.: American College Personnel Association, 1986. (Originally published 1937.)

Amundson, K. J. *Teaching Values and Ethics. American Association of School Administrators Critical Issues.* Report 24. Arlington, Va.: American Association of School Administrators, 1991.

Anton, T. "The Killing of Professor Culianu." *Lingua Franca,* Sept. 1992, pp. 1–8.

Astin, A. *Four Critical Years.* San Francisco: Jossey-Bass, 1977.

Astin, A. *Achieving Educational Excellence: A Critical Assessment of Priorities and Practices in Higher Education.* San Francisco: Jossey-Bass, 1985.

Astin, A. "Moral Messages of the University." *Educational Record,* 1989, *70,* 22–25.

Astin, A. "Higher Education and the Concept of Community." Fifteenth David Dodds Henry Lecture, University of Illinois, Champaign, Oct. 1993a.

Astin, A. *What Matters in College: Four Critical Years Revisited.* San Francisco: Jossey-Bass, 1993b.

Auden, W. H. "Today's 'Wonder-World' Needs Alice." *New York Times Magazine,* July 1, 1962, p. 5.

Bahm, A. J. *Axiology: The Science of Values.* Albuquerque, N.M.: World Books, 1980.

Baldwin, J. *The Price of the Ticket: Collected Nonfiction.* New York: St. Martin's/Marek, 1985.

Balogh, T. "Social Injustice and Rational Reform." In T.E.H. Reid (ed.), *Values in Conflict.* Toronto: University of Toronto Press, 1963.

Barrett, J. *Life of Abraham Lincoln, President of the United States.* New York: Moore, Wilstach, and Baldwin, 1865.

Becker, H. "Some Problems of Professionalism." *Adult Education,* 1956, *6,* 101–105.

Bell, T. "To Preserve the Blessings of Liberty." Text of Report on Stage Colleges' Role. *The Chronicle of Higher Education,* Nov. 12, 1986, p. 29–36.

Bellah, R. N., and others. *Habits of the Heart: Individualism and Commitment in American Life.* New York: HarperCollins, 1986.

Ben-David, J. *American Higher Education: Directions Old and New.* New York: McGraw-Hill, 1972.

Benne, K. "Art Education as the Development of Human Resources." In J. Brubacher (ed.), *Eclectic Philosophy of Education.* (2nd ed.) Englewood Cliffs, N.J.: Prentice Hall, 1962. (Originally published 1948.)

Bennett, W. *To Reclaim a Legacy.* Washington, D.C.: National Endowment for the Humanities, 1984.

Berger, J. *Ways of Seeing.* London: Penguin Books, 1972.

Bergquist, W. H. *The Four Cultures of the Academy: Insights and Strategies for Improving Leadership in Collegiate Organizations.* San Francisco: Jossey-Bass, 1992.

Bernays, A. "Art and the Morality of the Artist." *The Chronicle of Higher Education,* Jan. 1993, pp. B1–B2.

Berte, N. R., and O'Neil, E. H. "Old and New Models of Service." In W. B. Martin (ed.), *Redefining Service, Research, and Teaching.* New Directions for Higher Education, no. 18. San Francisco: Jossey-Bass, 1977.

Birnbaum, R. *How Colleges Work: The Cybernetics of Organization and Leadership.* San Francisco: Jossey-Bass, 1991.

Bloom, A. *The Closing of the American Mind.* New York: Simon & Schuster, 1987.

Bok, D. *Beyond the Ivory Tower: Social Responsibilities of the Modern University.* Cambridge, Mass.: Harvard University Press, 1982.

Boller, P. "William James as an Educator: Individualism and Democracy." In D. Sloan (ed.), *Education and Values.* New York: Teachers College Press, 1980.

Borelli, F. "The Art of Administration." *NASPA Journal* (National Association of Student Personnel Administrators), 1984, *22*(1), 14–16.

Bowen, H. R. *Investment in Learning: The Individual and Social Value of American Higher Education.* San Francisco: Jossey-Bass, 1977.

Boyer, E. L. *College: The Undergraduate Experience in America.* New York: HarperCollins, 1987.

Boyer, E. L. *Scholarship Reconsidered: Priorities of the Professoriate.* Princeton, N.J.: Carnegie Foundation for the Advancement of Teaching, 1990.

Bradford, J. A. "Policing the Movement of Modern Education." Paper presented at the annual meeting of the Midwest Sociological Society, Champaign, Ill., Apr. 1976.

Brandt, R. S. "Defending Public Education from the Neo-Puritans." *Educational Leadership,* May 1987, p. 3.

Brauer, C. "The Christian College in American Education." *The Christian Scholar,* 1958, *41,* 233–245.

Brazelton, B. Audiotaped conversation. In B. Moyers, *The National Soul,* Washington, D.C.: Mystic Fire Audio, Public Affairs Television, 1989.

Brown, R. *Student Development in Tomorrow's Higher Education—A Return to the Academy.* Washington, D.C.: American College Personnel Association, 1972.

Brown, R. D., and Krager, L. "Ethical Issues in Graduate Education. "*Journal of Higher Education,* 1985, *56*(4), 403–418.

Brubacher, J. S. (ed.). *Eclectic Philosophy of Education.* (2nd ed.) Englewood Cliffs, N.J.: Prentice Hall, 1962.

Brubacher, J. S. *Bases for Policy in Higher Education.* New York: McGraw-Hill, 1965.

Brubacher, J. S. *On the Philosophy of Higher Education.* San Francisco: Jossey-Bass, 1976.

Buber, M. *Between Man and Man.* New York: Macmillan, 1965.

Bundy, M. "An Atmosphere to Breathe: Woodrow Wilson and the Life of the American University College." In Woodrow Wilson Foundation, *Education in the Nation's Service.* New York: Praeger, 1960.

Burns, J. M. *Leadership.* New York: HarperCollins, 1978.

Caffrey, J. "Alternative Models." In G. Smith (ed.), *The Troubled Campus.* San Francisco: Jossey-Bass, 1970.

Campbell, J. *The Hero with a Thousand Faces.* New York: Meridian Books, 1949.

Campbell, J. *The Power of Myth: Conversations with Bill Moyers.* New York: Doubleday, 1988.

Campbell, J. *An Open Life: Conversations with Michael Toms.* New York: HarperCollins, 1989.

Capra, F. *The Tao of Physics.* New York: Bantam Books, 1975.

Carnegie Foundation for the Advancement of Teaching. *Campus Life: In Search of Community.* Princeton, N.J.: Carnegie Foundation for the Advancement of Teaching, 1990.

Carter, S. "The Insufficiency of Honesty." *Atlantic Monthly,* Feb. 1996, pp. 74–76.

Catford, L., and Ray, M. *The Path of the Everyday Hero.* New York: Tarcher/Putnam, 1991.

Chambers, C. "Foundations of Ethical Responsibility in Higher Education Administration." In M. C. Baca and R. H. Stein (eds.), *Professional Ethics in University Administration.* New Directions for Higher Education, no. 33. San Francisco, Jossey-Bass, 1981.

Clark, B. *The Open Door College: A Case Study.* New York: McGraw-Hill, 1960.

Clement, L. "Equality, Human Dignity, and Altruism." In R. Young (ed.), *Identifying and Implementing the Essential Values of the Profession.* New Directions for Student Services, no. 61. Jossey-Bass, 1993.

Clothier, R. "College Personnel Principles and Functions." In G. Saddlemire and A. Rentz (eds.), *Student Affairs: A Profession's Heritage.* Washington, D.C.: American College Personnel Association, Media Publication, no. 40, Revised Edition. (Originally published 1931.)

Cohen, A. *Dateline '79: Heretical Concepts for the Community College.* Beverly Hills, Calif.: Glencoe Press, 1969.

Coleman, J. R. *Blue Collar Journal: A College President's Sabbatical.* Philadelphia: Lippincott, 1974.

Committee on Freedom of Expression. C. Vann Woodward, Chair. *Final Report of the Committee on Freedom of Expression at Yale.* New Haven, Conn.: Yale University, 1975.

Conant, J. B. *Two Modes of Thought: My Encounters with Science and Education.* New York: Trident Press, 1964.

Cooley, C. *Social Organization.* New York: Schocken Books, 1962.

Cooper, S., and Savage, D. "CUNY, the Vocational University." *New York Times,* April 8, 1996, p. A16.

Cowley, W. H. "An Overview of American Colleges and Universities." Kent State University, 1961. (Mimeograph.)

Cowley, W. H. "The Nature of Student Personnel Work." In G. Saddlemire and A. Rentz (eds.), *Student Affairs: A Profession's Heritage.* Washington, D.C.: American College Personnel Association, Media Publication, no. 40, Revised Edition. (Originally published 1936.)

Croce, B. *The Essence of Aesthetic.* London: Heinemann, 1921.

Cross, K. P. *Adults as Learners: Increasing Participation and Facilitating Learning.* San Francisco: Jossey-Bass, 1981.

Culianu, I. "The Language of Creation." *Exquisite Corpse,* May 1991.

cummings, e. e. "A Poet's Advice to Students." In G. Firmage(ed.), *e. e. cummings: A Miscellany Revised.* New York: October House, 1965. (Originally published 1955.)

Danner, M. "Running Free." *New Yorker,* Mar. 4, 1996, p. 123.

Dass, R., and Gorman, P. *How Can I Help? Stories and Reflections on Service.* New York: Knopf, 1985.

De Unamuno, M. "The Man of Flesh and Bone." Reprinted in L. Michel and R. Sewall (eds.), *Tragedy: Modern Essays in Criticism.* Englewood Cliffs, N.J.: Prentice Hall, 1963.

de Winter Hebron, C. "In the 'Education Business,' Who Owns What?" *Higher Education in Europe,* 1993, *18*(1), 3–11.

Dewey, J. *A Common Faith.* New Haven, Conn.: Yale University Press, 1934.

Dillard, A. *Living by Fiction.* New York: HarperCollins, 1982.

Doctorow, E. L. Audiotaped conversation. In B. Moyers, *The National Soul.* Washington, D.C.: Mystic Fire Audio, Public Affairs Television, 1989.

Emerson, R. W. "Self Reliance." In R. W. Emerson, *Essays, Poems, and Addresses.* New York: Walter J. Black, 1941. (Originally published 1841.)

Ephland, J. "Why Play Standards?" *Down Beat,* Feb. 1996, pp. 16–20.

Erikson, E. *Identity: Youth and Crisis.* New York: Norton, 1968.

Estanek, S. "Definitions of Freedom: A Matrix for Decision Making." *NASPA Journal* (National Association of Student Personnel Administrators), Fall 1995, *33*(1), 65–71.

Etzioni, A. (ed.). *The Semi-Professions and Their Organization.* New York: Free Press, 1969.

Farago, J. M. "Academic Chivalry and Professional Responsibility." In M. C. Baca and R. H. Stein (eds.), *Professional Ethics in University Administration.* New Directions for Higher Education, no. 33. San Francisco: Jossey-Bass, 1981.

Feld, B. T. "On Legitimizing Public-Service Science in the University." *Daedalus,* 1975, *104*(1; special edition, *American Higher Education: Towards an Uncertain Future*), 244–247.

Ferguson, M. *The Aquarian Conspiracy: Personal and Social Transformation in the 1980s.* Los Angeles: Tarcher, 1980.

Fisher, M. B., and Noble, J. L. *College Education as Personal Development.* Englewood Cliffs, N.J.: Prentice Hall, 1960.

Flexner, A. *Daniel Coit Gilman, Creator of the American Type of University.* Orlando, Fla.: Harcourt Brace, 1946.

Folger, J. K. "Urban Sprawl in the Academic Community," *Journal of Higher Education,* Nov. 1963, p. 453.

Frankel, C. "Equality of Opportunity." *Ethics,* 1971, *81*, 199–211.

Frankel, C. "Facts, Values, and Responsible Choice." In S. Hook, P. Kurtz, and M. Todorovich (eds.), *The Ethics of Teaching and Scientific Research.* Buffalo, N.Y.: Prometheus Books, 1977.

Franzen, J. "First City." *New Yorker,* Feb. 19, 1996, pp. 85–92.

Freed, D. "Enduring Values from the Founding to the Present." Founder's Day Speech. Ada: Ohio Northern University, 1991.

Fulghum, R. *From Beginning to End: The Rituals of Our Lives.* New York: Ivy Books, 1995.

Galston, W. "Equality of Opportunity and Liberal Theory." In F. S. Lucash (ed.), *Justice and Equality Here and Now.* Ithaca, N.Y.: Cornell University Press, 1986.

Gardner, J. W. *Excellence: Can We Be Equal and Excellent Too?* New York: HarperCollins, 1961.

Gardner, J. W. "Creating Community in a Troubled World." In R. Kidder, *Shared Values for a Troubled World: Conversations with Men and Women of Conscience.* San Francisco: Jossey-Bass, 1994.

Gates, H. L. "The Charmer." *New Yorker,* Apr. 29/May 6, 1996, pp. 116–126.

Gee, G. "Land-Grant Colleges Ready for a Tuneup." *The Columbus Dispatch,* Apr. 15, 1996, p. C3.

Goodman, N. "Art and Inquiry." In M. Philipson and P. Gudel (eds.), *Aesthetics Today.* New York: New American Library, 1980.

Goodman, P. *The Community of Scholars.* New York: Vintage Books, 1964.

Greenberg, J. *I Never Promised You a Rose Garden.* Austin, Tex.: Holt, Rinehart and Winston, 1964.

Greene, G. *Monsignor Quixote.* London: Bodley Head Landing, 1982.

Hardin, G. *The Limits of Altruism: An Ecologist's View of Survival.* Bloomington: Indiana University Press, 1977.

Harrington, M. *The Politics at God's Funeral.* New York: Viking Penguin, 1983.

Harris, E. E. "Reason in Science and Conduct." In E. Laszlo and J. B. Wilbur (eds.), *Human Values and Natural Science.* New York: Gordon & Breach, 1970.

Hastings Center. *The Teaching of Ethics in Higher Education.* Hastings-on-Hudson, N.Y.: Hastings Center, 1980.

Henri, R. *The Art of Spirit.* New York: HarperCollins, 1923.

Hentoff, N. *Free Speech for Me But Not for Thee.* New York: HarperCollins, 1992.

Hesburgh, T. *The Hesburgh Papers: Higher Values in Higher Education.* Kansas City, Mo.: Andrews & McMeel, 1979.

Hodgkinson, H. "Students and an Intellectual Community." *Educational Record,* Fall 1968, p. 403.

Hofstadter, R. *Anti-Intellectualism in American Life.* New York: Vintage Books, 1963.

Hofstadter, R., and Metzger, W. *The Development of Academic Freedom in the United States.* New York: Columbia University Press, 1955.

Holland, B. "Making E Pluribus Unum Personal." *New York Times,* Jan. 17, 1996, pp. B1, B2.

Honan, W. "Watchword in Ivory Tower Is Silence." *Akron Beacon Journal,* Aug. 7, 1994, p. B20.

Hooker, M. "Facing our Challenges." *American Association for Higher Education Bulletin,* May 1991, *43*(9), 7–8.

Hoopes, T. *The Limits of Intervention.* New York: Van Rees Press, 1969.

Hutchins, R. "Morals, Religion, and Higher Education." Address at Western Michigan University, Kalamazoo, Oct. 25, 1949.

Hutchins, R. *The Higher Learning in America.* New Haven, Conn.: Yale University Press, 1967.

International Association of University Professors and Lecturers. *Declaration of Rights and Duties Inherent in Academic Freedom.* Sienna, Italy: IAUPL, 1982.

Jacob, P. E. "Student Values." In G. K. Smith (ed.), *1945–1970: Twenty-Five Years.* San Francisco: Jossey-Bass, 1970. (Originally published 1957.)

Jones, H. M. "The American Concept of Academic Freedom." In L. Joughin (ed.), *Academic Freedom and Tenure: A Handbook of the American Association of University Professors.* Madison: University of Wisconsin Press, 1967.

Judson, G. "Data Show College Pays for Lavish Spending," *New York Times,* Apr. 18, 1996, p. A18.

Junell, J. S. *Matters of Feeling: Values Education Reconsidered.* Bloomington, Ind.: Phi Delta Kappa Educational Foundation, 1979.

Kerr, C. *The Uses of the University.* Cambridge, Mass.: Harvard University Press, 1963.

Kerr, C. "Knowledge Ethics and the New Academic Culture." *Change,* Jan./Feb. 1994, pp. 9–15.

Kitchener, K. S. "Intuition, Critical Evaluation and Ethical Principles: The Foundation for Ethical Decisions in Counseling Psychology." *The Counseling Psychologist,* 1984, *12*(3), 43–55.

Kolb, D. A. *Experiential Learning: Experience as the Source of Learning and Development.* Englewood Cliffs, N.J.: Prentice Hall, 1984.

Komives, S. "Each Small College Has a Story to Tell." *Journal of College Student Personnel,* Jan. 1986, *27,* 13–15.

Krishnamurti, J. *Beauty, Pleasure, Sorrow, and Love.* Ojai Talks. San Francisco: HarperCollins, 1985.

Kuh, G. D., Schuh, J. H., Whitt, E. J., and Associates. *Involving Colleges: Successful Approaches to Student Learning and Development Outside the Classroom.* San Francisco: Jossey-Bass, 1991.

Lappe, F. M. *Rediscovering America's Values.* New York: Random House, 1989.

Leeson, T. *The Habit of Rivers.* New York: Lyons & Burford, 1994.

Lehmann-Haupt, C. "The Loss When Cream Can't Rise to the Top," *New York Times*, Sept. 26, 1994, p. B2.

Lemann, N. "Kicking in Groups," *Atlantic Monthly*, Apr. 1996, pp. 22–26.

Lerner, M. *Values in Education: Notes Toward a Values Philosophy.* Bloomington, Ind.: Phi Delta Kappa Educational Foundation, 1976.

LeShan, L., and Margenau, H. *Einstein's Space and Van Gogh's Sky: Physical Reality and Beyond.* New York: Collier Books, 1982.

Levine, A. *When Dreams and Heroes Died: A Portrait of Today's College Student.* San Francisco: Jossey-Bass, 1980.

Levine, A. *Handbook on Undergraduate Curriculum: Prepared for the Carnegie Council on Policy Studies in Higher Education.* San Francisco: Jossey-Bass, 1981.

Lewis, H. *A Question of Values: Six Ways We Make the Personal Choices That Shape Our Lives.* New York: HarperCollins, 1990.

Lloyd-Jones, E., and Smith, M. *Student Personnel Work as Deeper Teaching.* New York: HarperCollins, 1954.

Machiavelli, N. *The Prince.* New York: New American Library, 1980. (Originally published 1532.)

MacLean, N. *A River Runs Through It.* New York: Pocket Books, 1976.

Marling, K., and Wetenhall, J. "Patriotic Fervor and the Truth About Iwo Jima." *The Chronicle of Higher Education*, Sept. 29, 1993, p. A52.

Marsden, G. *The Soul of the American University.* New York: Oxford University Press, 1994.

Martin, W. B. *Alternative to Irrelevance.* Nashville, Tenn.: Abingdon Press, 1968.

Martin, W. B. "Education as Intervention." *Educational Record.* Winter 1969, p. 47.

Martin, W. B. "Service Through Ideas of Value." In W. B. Martin (ed.), *Redefining Service, Research, and Teaching.* New Directions for Higher Education, no. 18. San Francisco: Jossey-Bass, 1977a.

Martin, W. B. "Teaching, Research, and Service—But the Greatest of These Is Service." In W. B. Martin (ed), *Redefining Service, Research, and Teaching.* New Directions for Higher Education, no. 18. San Francisco: Jossey-Bass, 1977b.

Martin, W. B. *A College of Character.* San Francisco: Jossey-Bass, 1982.

McCloskey, D. "Bourgeois Virtue." *The American Scholar*, 1994, *63*(2), 177–191.

Millett, J. *The Academic Community.* New York: McGraw-Hill, 1962.

Montefiore, A. "Value." In B. Almond and B. Wilson (eds.), *Values: A Symposium.* Atlantic Highlands, N.J.: Humanities Press, 1988.

Morgan, G. *Images of Organizations.* Thousand Oaks, Calif.: Sage, 1986.

Morrill, R. L. *Teaching Values in College.* San Francisco: Jossey-Bass, 1981.

Morris, C. "Perceptions of Executive Level Administrators of Eighteen Wisconsin Private Liberal Arts Colleges Regarding the Essential Values at Their Institutions." Unpublished doctoral dissertation, Department of Education, Kent State University, 1994.

Morrison, T. *Lecture and Speech of Acceptance Upon the Award of the Nobel Prize for Literature.* New York: Random House Audio Publishing, 1993.

Muelder, W. "Empowerment and the Integrity of Higher Education." In D. Robertson (ed.), *Power and Empowerment in Higher Education.* Lexington, Ky.: University Press of Kentucky, 1978.

Murphy, J. P. *Values in Catholic Higher Education: A Preliminary Report of a National Study.* Chicago: DePaul University, 1990.

Newman, F., and Oliver, D. "Education as Community." In C. Brembeck and M. Grandstaff (eds.), *Social Foundations of Education.* New York: Wiley, 1969.

Newman, J. *The Idea of a University.* Garden City, N.Y.: Image Books, 1959. (Originally published 1853.)

Page, C. "Road to Equality Served Better by Protecting First Amendment Rights, Not Restricting Them." *The Athens Post,* Oct. 8, 1993, p. 2.

Palmer, P. J. "Community Conflict and Ways of Knowing." *Change,* Sept./Oct. 1987, pp. 20–25.

Park, J. C. "The Religious Right and Public Education." *Educational Leadership,* May 1987, pp. 5–10.

Pascale, R., and Athos, A. *The Art of Japanese Management.* New York: Simon & Schuster, 1981.

Patterson, D. *When Learned Men Murder.* Bloomington, Ind.: Phi Delta Kappa Educational Foundation, 1996.

Pavela, G. "Editor's Column." *ACPA Commission XV News,* June 1984, pp. 1–4.

Pfaff, W. "On the Death of Mitterand." *New York Review of Books,* Feb. 15, 1996, p. 41.

President's Commission on Higher Education for Democracy. "Report of the President's Commission on Higher Education for Democracy." In L. Goodchild and H. Wechsler (eds.), *The History of Higher Education.* Needham Heights, Mass.: Ginn Press, 1989. (Originally published 1947.)

Quie, A. "The Tyranny of the Urgent." In *The Third Century: Twenty-Six Prominent Americans Speculate on the Educational Future.* New Rochelle, N.Y.: Change Magazine Press, 1977.

Raths, L., Harmin, M., and Simon, S. *Values and Teaching: Working with Values in the Classroom.* Columbus, Ohio: Merrill, 1966.

Redfield, R. "The Folk Society." In T. Lasswell (ed.), *Life in Society.* Glenview, Ill.: Scott, Foresman, 1965.

Remley, A. "Real vs. Ideal—A Response." *Journal of College Student Personnel,* Jan. 1986, *27,* 16–17.

Rheingold, H. *They Have a Word for It.* Los Angeles: Tarcher, 1988.

Riesman, D., Gusfield, J., and Gamson, Z. *Academic Values and Mass Education: The Early Years of Oakland and Monteith.* Garden City, N.Y.: Doubleday, Anchor Books, 1971.

Robbins, T. "Meditations on a Camel Pack." *Esquire,* July 1980, pp. 27–38.

Roberts, D. "Community: The Value of Social Synergey." In R. Young (ed.), *Identifying and Implementing the Essential Values of the Profession.* New Directions for Student Services, no. 61. San Francisco: Jossey-Bass, 1993.

Rogers, W. R. "Values in Higher Education." In C. T. Mitchell (ed.), *Values in Teaching and Professional Ethics.* Macon, Ga.: Mercer University Press, 1989.

Rosen, L. "The Old Bawl Game." *Men's Health,* Apr. 1996, pp. 58, 63.

Rothenberg, P. "Critics of Attempts to Democratize the Curriculum Are Waging a Campaign to Misrepresent the Work of Responsible Professors." *The Chronicle of Higher Education,* Apr. 10, 1991, pp. B1, B3.

Rothkopf, A. "CUNY Vocational Friction Has National Echo." *New York Times,* Apr. 13, 1996, p. A14.

Rudolph, F. *The American College and University.* New York: Knopf, 1962.

Sanchez, G. "The Autonomy of the University." *School and Society,* Mar. 19, 1966, p. 147.

Sandberg, P. "Response." Fifteenth David Dodds Henry Lecture, University of Illinois, Champaign, Oct. 1993.

Sanford, N. *Learning After College.* Orinda, Calif.: Montaigne, 1980.

Schlossberg, N. "Marginality and Mattering: Key Issues in Building Community." In D. Roberts (ed.), *Designing Campus Activities to Foster a Sense of Community.* New Directions for Student Services, no. 48. San Francisco: Jossey-Bass, 1989.

Schön, D. *Educating the Reflective Practitioner: Toward a New Design for Teaching and Learning in the Professions.* San Francisco: Jossey-Bass, 1987.

Sherrington, C. *Man on His Nature.* Cambridge, England: Cambridge University Press, 1940.

Shoemaker, F. *Aesthetic Experience and the Humanities: Modern Ideas of Aesthetic Experience in the Reading of World Literature.* New York: Columbia University Press, 1943.

Shoemaker, N. "Teaching the Truth About the History of the American West." *The Chronicle of Higher Education,* Oct. 27, 1993, p. A48.

Skaggs, W. "Work Values of Faculty Members in Selected Small Liberal Arts Colleges: A Comparative Study." Paper read at the annual conference of the Association for the Study of Higher Education, Baltimore, Nov. 1987.

Skinner, B. F. *Beyond Freedom and Dignity.* New York: Knopf, 1972.

Slaughter, S. "Academic Freedom and the State." *Journal of Higher Education,* 1988, *59*(3), 241–262.

Sloan D. "The Teaching of Ethics in the American Undergraduate Curriculum, 1876–1976." In D. Sloan (ed.), *Education and Values.* New York: Teachers College Press, 1980.

Smith, A. *An Inquiry into the Nature and Causes of the Wealth of Nations.* New York: Penguin Books, 1986. (Originally published 1776.)

Smith, D. "Values and Institutional Decision Making." *Academe,* 1985, *71*(6), 14–18.

Smith, D., and Reynolds, C. "Institutional Culture and Ethics." In W. W. May (ed.), *Ethics and Higher Education.* New York: American Council on Education/Macmillan, 1990.

Smith, T. V. "Middle-Sized Values." In G. K. Smith (ed.), *1945–1970: Twenty-Five Years.* San Francisco: Jossey-Bass, 1970.

Smith, W. *Professors and Public Ethics: Studies of Northern Moral Philosophers Before the Civil War.* Ithaca, N.Y.: Cornell University Press, 1956.

Solomon, R., and Solomon, J. *Up the University: Re-Creating Higher Education in America.* Reading, Mass.: Addison-Wesley, 1993.

Stamatakos, L. "Student Affairs Progress Toward Professionalism: Recommendations for Action." *Journal of College Student Personnel,* 1981, *22,* 105–111, 197–206.

Stimpson, C. R. "A Conversation, Not a Monologue." *The Chronicle of Higher Education,* Mar. 16, 1994, pp. B1–B2.

Stott, W. "The Role of Student Affairs in Values Education." In M. Collins (ed.), *Teaching Values and Ethics in College.* New Directions for Teaching and Learning, no. 13. San Francisco: Jossey-Bass, 1983.

Study Group on the Conditions of Excellence in American Higher Education. *Involvement in Learning: Realizing the Potential of American Higher Education.* Washington, D.C.: National Institute of Education, 1984.

Sykes, C. H. *ProfScam: Professors and the Demise of Higher Education.* New York: St. Martin's Press, 1988.

"Taken at Their Word." *New York Times* (national ed.), Feb. 14, 1994, p. B1.

Taylor, H. "Progressive Philosophy." In G. K. Smith (ed.), *1945–1970: Twenty-Five Years.* San Francisco: Jossey-Bass, 1970.

Terenzini, P., and Pascarella, E. "Living with the Myths: Undergraduate Education in America," *Change,* Jan./Feb. 1994, pp. 28–32.

"The Terrible and Sacred Shore." *New York Times,* June 6, 1994, p. A10.

Tillich, P. *The Courage to Be.* New Haven, Conn.: Yale University Press, 1952.

Tillich, P. *My Travel Diary: 1936, Between Two Worlds.* New York: HarperCollins, 1970.

Tollefson, A. *New Approaches to College Student Development.* New York: Behavioral Publications, 1975.

Tozer, S. "Response." Fifteenth David Dodds Henry Lecture, University of Illinois, Champaign, Oct. 1993.

Trachtenberg, S. "Presidents Can Establish a Moral Tone on Campus." *Educational Record,* 1989, *70*(2), 4–9.

Trow, M. "Higher Education and Moral Development." *AAUP Bulletin,* 1976, *62*(1), 20–27.

Turnbull, W. "Integrity." *USA Weekend,* Nov. 17, 1995, p. 10.

Upcraft, M. L. "Managing Right." In M. L. Upcraft and M. J. Barr (eds.), *Managing Student Affairs Effectively.* New Directions for Student Services, no. 41. San Francisco: Jossey-Bass, 1988.

U.S. News and World Report. *America's Best Colleges.* U.S. News and World Report, 1994.

Vaill, P. *Managing as a Performing Art: New Ideas for a World of Chaotic Change.* San Francisco: Jossey-Bass, 1991.

Van Patten, J. "The Case for the Individual Man in the Educational Environment." *School and Society,* Apr. 1, 1967, p. 232.

Vaughan, G. (ed.). *Questioning the Community College Role.* New Directions for Community Colleges, no. 32. San Francisco: Jossey-Bass, 1980.

Veblen, T. *The Higher Learning in America: A Memorandum on the Conduct of Universities by Business Men.* New York: Hill & Wang, 1957. (Originally published 1918.)

Vlastos, G. "Justice and Equality." In R. B. Brandt (ed.), *Social Injustice.* Englewood Cliffs, N.J.: Prentice Hall, 1962.

Walker, D. "The President as Ethical Leader of the Campus. In M. C. Baca and R. H. Stein, (eds.), *Professional Ethics in University Administration.* New Directions for Higher Education, no. 33. San Francisco: Jossey-Bass, 1981.

Wernick, R. "Conspiracy Theorists, Reveal Thyselves." *Smithsonian,* Mar. 1994, *24*(12), 108–124.

Whitely, J., Bertin, B., Ferrant, E., and Yokota, N. "Influences of Character Development During the College Years." In J. Dalton (ed.), *Promoting Values Development in College Students.* NASPA Monograph, no. 4. Washington, D.C.: National Association of Student Personnel Administrators, 1985.

Wicker, C. "New Book Defines 'Integrity' as a Journey, Not a Destination." *Columbus Dispatch,* Apr. 14, 1996, pp. I20–I21.

Wiggins, D. *Needs, Values, Truth: Essays in the Philosophy of Value.* Vol. 1: *Aristotelian Society Series.* (2nd ed.) Cambridge, Mass.: Blackwell, 1991.

Williams, D., Klein, S., and Foote, D. "The Trickle Down Effect." *Newsweek,* Sept. 20, 1982, p. 64.

Williamson, E. G. *Trends in Student Personnel Work*. Minneapolis: University of Minnesota Press, 1949.

Wilson, D. "Thomas Jefferson and the Character Issue." *The Atlantic*, 1992, *270*(5), 57–75.

Wilson, J. "Values in Education." In B. Almond and B. Wilson (eds), *Values: A Symposium*. Atlantic Highlands, N.J.: Humanities Press, 1988.

Wireman, B. "Modern University's Greatest Need: A Vision of Its Own End." *Peabody Journal of Education*, July 1967, p. 35.

Withers, A. "Perceptions of Academic Department Chairs at Twelve Ohio Private, Liberal Arts Colleges Regarding the Essential Values at Their Institutions." Unpublished doctoral dissertation, Department of Education, Kent State University, 1993.

Woodford, J. "Dalai Lama Delivers Wallenberg Lecture." *Michigan Today*. June 6, 1994, p. 2.

Wrenn, C., and Darley, J. "Appraisal of the Professional Status of Student Personnel Work." In E. Williamson (ed.), *Trends in Student Personnel Work*. Minneapolis: University of Minnesota Press, 1949.

Ylvisaker, P. "Promoting Social Justice: From the Campus to the Community." *Educational Record*, Fall 1990, *71*(4), 15–18.

Young, R. B., and Elfrink, V. L. "Essential Values of Student Affairs Work." *Journal of College Student Development*, 1990, *32*, 47–55.

Young, R. E. "Faculty Development and the Concept of 'Profession.'" *Academe*, May/June 1987, pp. 12–14.

Zukav, G. *The Dancing Wu Li Masters*. Los Angeles: Audio Renaissance Tapes, 1990.

Zwerling, S. *Second Best*. N.Y.: McGraw-Hill, 1976.

Williamson, J. N. *New Survival Strategies.* N.Y.: Minneapolis: Curtis and Ginn. Inc. [etc.], 1919.

Wilson, Ian. *Those Years and Into the Future.* [etc.]: N.Y.: [etc.], 1982. [etc.], 25-36.

Witham, L. *Values and the Future.* In E. Almquist and R. Wilson (eds.), *The New Dynamics.* Atlantic Highlands, N.J.: Humanities Press, 1989.

Wiseman, D. *Modern University Organization.* by Virginia A. Owen Finch (ed.) [etc.]: N.Y.: [etc.], 1993. [etc.]

Wolff, L. A. "Perception of Meaning in Organizational Change." Ph.D. diss., Union Theological College. For finding the *Accepted Values*. Reproduction as Unpublished doctoral dissertation. Department of Organizational Studies. University. Minnesota, 1993.

Woodard, J. "Trends and Beliefs." *Management Forecast.* Michigan Free Press, 1991. 9-27.

Wrenn, C. "An Analysis." *Appraisal of the Character and Status of Students." Personal Service." In Williamson (ed.), *The Assessor Program.* N.N. Minneapolis: University of Minnesota Press, 1949.

Wyatt, J. R. "Promotions Social Justice: From the Margin to the Center." [etc.]: Anthropology Forum. Fall 1994. 20(4), 16-23.

Young, R. E. and Thind, V. J. *Teaching Values: Selected Readings.* Boston: College Search. Reissued, 1990. 78-257.

Young, T. G. "Ethics Development and the Culture of Professions." [etc.]: [etc.], June 1987. pp. 18-24.

Zelan, G. P. *Downsizing.* Los Angeles: UCLA Angelo Resistance Press. 1990.

Zweitling, Moore, & K. *Not the Organization.* [etc.], 1991.

Name Index

Subject Index

DATE DUE

OhioLINK   MAY 20

LA 227.4 .Y68 1997

Young, Robert B.

No neutral ground